Half Baked Harvest cookbook

A Collection of Deliciously Inventive Recipes and Culinary Adventures

BY Esme Rada

TABLE OF CONTENTS

Introduction 5

Breakfast Recipes 6

   Lemon Ricotta Pancakes with Blueberry Sauce 6

   Chai-Spiced French Toast with Caramelized Apples 8

   Breakfast Quesadillas with Soft Scrambled Eggs and Avocado..... 10

   Savory Sweet Potato Breakfast Bowls with Soft-Boiled Eggs 11

   Nutella-Stuffed Banana Bread French Toast 13

   Coconut Mango Smoothie Bowls with Granola 14

   Greek Yogurt Pancakes with Raspberry Compote 15

   Huevos Rancheros Breakfast Tacos with Avocado Crema 17

   Maple Pecan Baked Oatmeal with Caramelized Bananas 19

   Smoked Salmon Breakfast Croissants with Herbed Cream Cheese
.... 21

   Breakfast Burrito Bowls with Spicy Black Beans and Fried Eggs . 22

Cinnamon Roll Dutch Baby with Cream Cheese Glaze 24

   Breakfast Pizza with Eggs, Bacon, and Roasted Tomatoes 26

   Blueberry Lemon Ricotta Pancakes with Blueberry Compote 27

   Savoury Spinach and Feta Galette with a Soft-Boiled Egg 29

   Nutella Swirl Banana Bread French Toast Sticks 31

   Coconut Berry Smoothie Bowl with Toasted Coconut Granola 33

   Breakfast Tacos with Spicy Chorizo and Scrambled Eggs 35

   Caramelized Pear Dutch Baby with Whipped Mascarpone 37

Caprese Avocado Toast with Balsamic Glaze 39

Lunch Recipes: 41

Thai Peanut Chicken and Veggie Spring Rolls with Sweet Chili Sauce 41

Grilled Peach and Prosciutto Pizza with Honey Balsamic Glaze ... 42

Harvest Cobb Salad with Honey Mustard Vinaigrette.................. 44

BBQ Chicken Quinoa Salad with Avocado and Lime 46

Mediterranean Hummus Bowl with Herbed Pita Chips 47

California Turkey Club Wrap with Avocado Ranch Dressing 49

Spicy Shrimp Sushi Bowls with Creamy Sriracha Sauce 51

Greek Salad with Grilled Chicken and Tzatziki Dressing.............. 53

Caprese Pesto Pasta Salad with Balsamic Glaze 55

Veggie Sushi Rolls with Spicy Sriracha Mayo 56

Roasted Vegetable Panzanella Salad with Balsamic Glaze 58

Thai Coconut Chicken and Rice Noodle Soup 59

California Chicken, Avocado, and Bacon Salad with Tahini Dressing 61

Mediterranean Veggie Wraps with Sun-Dried Tomato Hummus . 63

Caprese Orzo Pasta Salad with Basil Vinaigrette......................... 65

Grilled Peach, Corn, and Avocado Salad with Honey Lime Vinaigrette... 66

Buffalo Chicken Lettuce Wraps with Blue Cheese Dressing 68

Vietnamese Banh Mi Sandwiches with Pickled Vegetables 70

Roasted Tomato and Basil Pesto Grilled Cheese Sandwiches....... 73

Chipotle Chicken and Avocado Quinoa Salad with Honey Lime Vinaigrette 74

Dinner Recipes 77

One-pan Moroccan Chicken with Couscous and Chickpeas 77

Creamy Garlic Butter Tuscan Shrimp with Spinach and Sun-Dried Tomatoes 78

Sheet Pan Honey Garlic Chicken and Veggies 80

Spaghetti Carbonara with Crispy Prosciutto and Peas 82

Honey Sriracha Glazed Salmon with Sesame Noodles 84

Cajun Shrimp and Grits with Andouille Sausage 86

Teriyaki Chicken Stir-Fry with Vegetables and Rice 88

Creamy Sun-Dried Tomato Chicken Parmesan 89

Beef and Broccoli Ramen Stir-Fry with Garlic Butter Sauce 91

Caprese Stuffed Chicken with Balsamic Glaze 93

Garlic Butter Mushroom Risotto with Peas and Parmesan 95

One-Pot Creamy Lemon Chicken and Asparagus Orzo 97

Chipotle Lime Salmon Tacos with Mango Salsa 98

Creamy Spinach and Artichoke Stuffed Chicken 100

Spicy Sausage and Pepperoni Pizza with Garlic Butter Crust 102

Thai Coconut Peanut Chicken Satay with Spicy Peanut Sauce 104

Honey Garlic Butter Shrimp and Broccoli with Rice 106

Balsamic Glazed Steak Rolls with Provolone and Basil 108

Creamy Lemon Garlic Butter Salmon with Asparagus 109

Pesto Chicken and Summer Vegetable Sheet Pan Gnocchi 111

Conclusion 114

INTRODUCTION

Welcome to the world of Half-Baked Harvest! In this cookbook, I invite you to embark on a culinary adventure filled with deliciously inventive recipes and inspiring flavours. Whether you're a seasoned home cook or just starting your culinary journey, there's something here for everyone. Join me as we explore the joys of cooking with fresh, seasonal ingredients and creating memorable meals that delight your taste buds and nourish your soul. Get ready to roll up your sleeves, fire up the stove, and let your creativity run wild in the kitchen. Let's make some magic happen!

BREAKFAST RECIPES

LEMON RICOTTA PANCAKES WITH BLUEBERRY SAUCE

Cooking Time: 20 minutes

Servings: 4

Ingredients:

For the pancakes:

- 1 cup all-purpose flour
- One tablespoon sugar
- One teaspoon of baking powder
- 1/2 teaspoon baking soda
- 1/4 teaspoon salt
- 1 cup ricotta cheese
- Two large eggs
- 1/2 cup milk
- Zest of 1 lemon
- Two tablespoons of lemon juice
- Butter or oil for cooking

For the blueberry sauce:

- 1 1/2 cups fresh or frozen blueberries
- 1/4 cup water
- Two tablespoons sugar
- One tablespoon of lemon juice
- One teaspoon of cornstarch mixed with one tablespoon of water (optional for thickening)

Steps:

1. **Prepare the Pancake Batter:** In a large bowl, whisk together the flour, sugar, baking powder, baking soda, and salt. Mix the ricotta cheese, eggs, milk, lemon zest, and lemon juice in another bowl until well combined. Pour the wet ingredients into the dry ingredients and stir until just combined. Be careful not to overmix; some lumps are okay.

2. **Cook the Pancakes:** Heat a skillet or griddle over medium heat and add a small amount of butter or oil. Pour about 1/4 cup of batter onto the skillet for each pancake. Cook until bubbles form on the surface of the pancake and the edges look set, about 2-3 minutes. Flip and cook for 1-2 minutes or until golden brown. Repeat with the remaining batter, adding more butter or oil to the skillet as needed.

3. **Make the Blueberry Sauce:** In a small saucepan, combine the blueberries, water, sugar, and lemon juice. Bring to a simmer over medium heat, stirring occasionally. Cook until the blueberries burst and the sauce thickens slightly about 5-7 minutes. If desired, stir in the cornstarch mixture and cook for 1-2 minutes until thickening.

4. **Serve:** Stack the pancakes on plates and spoon the warm blueberry sauce over the top. Serve immediately.

Nutrition Facts (per serving):

- Calories: 320
- Total Fat: 10g
    - Saturated Fat: 5g
    - Trans Fat: 0g
- Cholesterol: 120mg
- Sodium: 480mg
- Total Carbohydrate: 47g
    - Dietary Fiber: 2g
    - Sugars: 15g
- Protein: 12g

CHAI-SPICED FRENCH TOAST WITH CARAMELIZED APPLES

Cooking Time: 20 minutes

Servings: 4

Materials:

- Eight slices of thick-cut bread (such as brioche or challah)
- Four large eggs
- 1 cup milk
- Two teaspoons of vanilla extract
- Two teaspoons of ground cinnamon
- One teaspoon of ground ginger
- 1/2 teaspoon ground cardamom
- 1/4 teaspoon ground cloves
- 1/4 teaspoon ground nutmeg
- Two tablespoons butter
- Two apples, peeled, cored, and thinly sliced
- 1/4 cup brown sugar
- Maple syrup for serving
- Optional toppings: whipped cream, chopped nuts

Steps:

1. In a shallow bowl, whisk together the eggs, milk, vanilla extract, and all the spices until well combined.

2. Heat a large skillet or griddle over medium heat and add one tablespoon of butter, allowing it to melt and coat the surface.

3. Dip each slice of bread into the egg mixture, ensuring both sides are well-coated but not soggy.

4. Place the coated bread slices onto the heated skillet or griddle and cook until golden brown on each side, about 2-3 minutes per side. Cook in batches if necessary, adding more butter to the skillet.

5. While the French toast is cooking, prepare the caramelized apples. Melt the remaining tablespoon of butter over medium heat in a separate skillet.

6. Add the sliced apples and brown sugar to the skillet, stirring to coat the apples evenly with the sugar.

7. Cook the apples, stirring occasionally, until they are tender and caramelized, about 5-7 minutes.

8. Once the French toast is cooked and the apples are caramelized, serve the French toast topped with the caramelized apples.

9. Drizzle with maple syrup and add optional toppings, whipped cream or chopped nuts, if desired.

10. Serve immediately and enjoy your delicious Chai-Spiced French Toast with Caramelized Apples!

Nutrition Facts (per serving):

- Calories: 360
- Total Fat: 14g
- Saturated Fat: 7g
- Cholesterol: 195mg
- Sodium: 330mg
- Total Carbohydrates: 48g
- Dietary Fiber: 3g
- Sugars: 24g
- Protein: 12g

BREAKFAST QUESADILLAS WITH SOFT SCRAMBLED EGGS AND AVOCADO

Cooking Time: 15 minutes

Serving: 2

Materials:

- Four large eggs
- Two large tortillas
- One ripe avocado, sliced
- 1 cup shredded cheddar cheese
- One tablespoon butter
- Salt and pepper to taste
- Optional: salsa, sour cream, or hot sauce for serving

Steps:

1. **Prepare Eggs:** Cut the eggs into a bowl and lightly beat them with a fork. Season with salt and pepper to taste. Heat a non-stick skillet over medium-low heat and add butter. Once the butter is melted, pour in the beaten eggs. Gently scramble the eggs until they are set but still soft and slightly runny. Remove from heat and set aside.

2. **Assemble Quesadillas:** Lay out the tortillas on a clean surface. Divide the scrambled eggs evenly between the two tortillas, spreading them in a single layer. Top the eggs with sliced avocado and shredded cheddar cheese.

3. **Cook Quesadillas:** Heat a large skillet or griddle over medium heat. Carefully transfer one assembled quesadilla to the skillet and cook until the bottom tortilla is golden brown and crispy, and the cheese is melted, about 2-3 minutes. A spatula folds the quesadilla in

half and then transfers it to a cutting board. Repeat with the remaining quesadilla.

4. **Slice and Serve:** Let the quesadillas cool for a minute, then use a sharp knife to slice each quesadilla into wedges. Serve hot with salsa, sour cream, or hot sauce on the side.

Nutrition Facts (per serving):

- Calories: 482 kcal
- Total Fat: 32g
    - Saturated Fat: 13g
    - Trans Fat: 0g
- Cholesterol: 389mg
- Sodium: 649mg
- Total Carbohydrates: 28g
    - Dietary Fiber: 8g
    - Sugars: 1g
- Protein: 22g

SAVORY SWEET POTATO BREAKFAST BOWLS WITH SOFT-BOILED EGGS

Cooking Time: 30 minutes

Serving: 2

Materials:

- Two medium sweet potatoes peeled and cubed
- Four large eggs
- One avocado, sliced
- 1 cup cherry tomatoes, halved
- 2 cups baby spinach
- One tablespoon of olive oil

- Salt and pepper to taste
- Optional toppings: crumbled feta cheese, chopped chives, hot sauce

Steps:

1. **Prepare the Sweet Potatoes:** Place the cubed sweet potatoes in a microwave-safe bowl. Cover with a damp paper towel and microwave on high for 5-7 minutes, or until tender.

2. **Soft-Boil the Eggs:** Bring a pot of water to a boil. Gently lower the eggs into the boiling water using a spoon. Cook for 6 minutes for soft-boiled eggs. Remove the eggs with a slotted spoon and transfer them to a bowl of ice water to stop cooking. Once cool, carefully peel the eggs and set aside.

3. **Sauté the Spinach:** Heat olive oil over medium heat in a skillet. Add baby spinach and sauté until wilted, about 2-3 minutes. Season with salt and pepper to taste.

4. **Assemble the Bowls:** Divide the cooked sweet potatoes, sautéed spinach, sliced avocado, and halved cherry tomatoes between two serving bowls.

5. **Add Soft-Boiled Eggs:** Carefully slice the soft-boiled eggs in half and place them on top of the assembled bowls.

6. **Optional Toppings:** Sprinkle with crumbled feta cheese and chopped chives, and drizzle with hot sauce if desired.

7. **Serve:** Serve immediately and enjoy a nutritious and delicious breakfast!

Nutrition Facts (per serving):

- Calories: 340
- Total Fat: 19g

- Saturated Fat: 4g
- Trans Fat: 0g
- Cholesterol: 186mg
- Sodium: 179mg
- Total Carbohydrates: 34g
  - Dietary Fiber: 10g
  - Sugars: 7g
- Protein: 12g

NUTELLA-STUFFED BANANA BREAD FRENCH TOAST

Cooking Time: 30 minutes

Servings: 4

Materials:

- One loaf of banana bread (store-bought or homemade)
- Nutella (as much as desired)
- Four large eggs
- 1/2 cup milk
- One teaspoon of vanilla extract
- Butter or cooking spray for greasing the pan
- Powdered sugar (optional for dusting)
- Sliced bananas and berries (optional, for garnish)

Steps:

1. **Prepare the Banana Bread:** Slice the banana bread into thick slices, about 1-inch thick. Then, using a sharp knife, carefully cut a slit in the middle of each slice, creating a pocket for the Nutella.

2. **Stuff with Nutella:** Take a generous amount of Nutella and stuff it into the slit of each banana bread slice. Make sure to spread it evenly inside.

3. **Prepare Egg Mixture:** In a shallow dish, whisk together the eggs, milk, and vanilla extract until well combined.

4. **Dip and Soak:** Heat a skillet or griddle over medium heat and grease it with butter or cooking spray. Dip each stuffed banana bread slice into the egg mixture, allowing it to soak for a few seconds on each side.

5. **Cook French Toast:** Place the soaked banana bread slices onto the hot skillet or griddle. Cook for 2-3 minutes on each side until golden brown and crispy.

6.**Serve:** Once cooked, transfer the Nutella-stuffed banana bread French toast to serving plates. Dust with powdered sugar if desired, and garnish with sliced bananas and berries.

Nutrition Facts (per serving):

- Calories: 380
- Total Fat: 18g
    - Saturated Fat: 6g
    - Trans Fat: 0g
- Cholesterol: 185mg
- Sodium: 370mg
- Total Carbohydrate: 46g
    - Dietary Fiber: 2g
    - Sugars: 25g
- Protein: 10g

COCONUT MANGO SMOOTHIE BOWLS WITH GRANOLA

Cooking Time: 10 minutes

Serving: 2 bowls

Materials:

- Two ripe mangoes, peeled and chopped
- 1 cup coconut milk
- 1/2 cup plain Greek yogurt
- Two tablespoons honey
- 1/2 cup granola
- 1/4 cup shredded coconut
- Sliced mango for garnish
- Fresh berries, for garnish

Steps:

1. combine the chopped mangoes, coconut milk, Greek yoghurt, and honey in a blender. Blend until smooth and creamy.

2. Pour the smoothie mixture into two bowls.

3. Top each bowl with granola, shredded coconut, sliced mango, and fresh berries.

4. Serve immediately and enjoy!

Nutrition Facts (per serving):

- Calories: 320
- Total Fat: 15g
- Saturated Fat: 10g
- Cholesterol: 3mg
- Sodium: 50mg
- Total Carbohydrate: 45g
- Dietary Fiber: 6g
- Sugars: 30g
- Protein: 6g

GREEK YOGURT PANCAKES WITH RASPBERRY COMPOTE

Cooking Time: 20 minutes

Servings: 4

Ingredients:

- 1 cup all-purpose flour
- One teaspoon of baking powder
- 1/2 teaspoon baking soda
- 1/4 teaspoon salt
- 1 cup Greek yogurt
- 1/4 cup milk
- Two large eggs
- Two tablespoons honey
- One teaspoon of vanilla extract
- One tablespoon of butter or oil for cooking

For Raspberry Compote:

- 2 cups fresh raspberries
- 1/4 cup water
- Two tablespoons honey
- One teaspoon of lemon juice

Steps:

1. **Prepare the Raspberry Compote:** In a small saucepan, combine the raspberries, water, honey, and lemon juice. Cook over medium heat, stirring occasionally, until the raspberries break down and the mixture thickens slightly, about 10-12 minutes. Remove from heat and set aside.

2. **Make the Pancake Batter:** In a large mixing bowl, whisk together the flour, baking powder, baking soda, and salt.

3. Mix the Greek yogurt, milk, eggs, honey, and vanilla extract in another bowl until well combined.

4. Pour the wet ingredients into the dry ingredients and stir until combined. Be careful not to overmix; it's okay if there are a few lumps.

5. **Cook the Pancakes:** Heat a non-stick skillet or griddle over medium heat and add a small amount of butter or oil.

6. Pour about 1/4 cup of batter onto the skillet for each pancake. Cook until bubbles form on the surface of the pancake and the edges begin to set about 2-3 minutes.

7. Flip the pancakes and cook for 1-2 minutes or until golden brown and cooked through.

8. **Serve:** Stack the pancakes on plates and spoon the raspberry compote over the top. Serve immediately.

Nutrition Facts (per serving):

- Calories: 290 kcal
- Total Fat: 7g
- Saturated Fat: 3g
- Cholesterol: 103mg
- Sodium: 415mg
- Total Carbohydrate: 46g
- Dietary Fiber: 4g
- Sugars: 18g
- Protein: 11g

HUEVOS RANCHEROS BREAKFAST TACOS WITH AVOCADO CREMA

Cooking Time: 25 minutes

Serving: 4 tacos

Materials:

- Four corn tortillas
- Four large eggs
- 1 cup cooked black beans
- 1 cup salsa
- One avocado, sliced
- 1/4 cup chopped fresh cilantro
- 1/4 cup crumbled queso fresco
- Salt and pepper to taste

For Avocado Crema:

- One ripe avocado
- 1/4 cup sour cream
- One tablespoon of lime juice
- Salt to taste

Steps:

1. **Prepare the Avocado Crema:** In a blender or food processor, combine the ripe avocado, sour cream, lime juice, and a pinch of salt. Blend until smooth and creamy. Transfer to a bowl and set aside.

2. **Warm the Tortillas:** Heat a non-stick skillet over medium heat. Warm the corn tortillas for about 30 seconds on each side until they are pliable and warm. Keep them warm by wrapping them in a clean kitchen towel.

3. **Cook the Eggs:** In the same skillet, crack the eggs and cook to your desired doneness. Season with salt and pepper.

4. **Assemble the Tacos:** Place a warmed tortilla on a plate. Spread a spoonful of black beans onto the tortilla. Top with a cooked egg, a dollop of salsa, and a few slices of avocado. Sprinkle with chopped cilantro and crumbled queso fresco.

5. **Serve:** Repeat with the remaining tortillas and ingredients. Serve the tacos immediately with the prepared avocado crema on the side.

Nutrition Facts (per serving):

- Calories: 280
- Total Fat: 15g
- Saturated Fat: 4g
- Cholesterol: 185mg
- Sodium: 420mg
- Total Carbohydrate: 24g
- Dietary Fiber: 7g
- Sugars: 2g
- Protein: 13g

MAPLE PECAN BAKED OATMEAL WITH CARAMELIZED BANANAS

Cooking Time: 45 minutes

Serving: 6

Materials:

- 2 cups rolled oats
- 1/2 cup chopped pecans
- One teaspoon baking powder
- 1/2 teaspoon ground cinnamon
- 1/4 teaspoon salt
- 2 cups milk (dairy or plant-based)
- 1/2 cup pure maple syrup
- Two large eggs
- Two tablespoons unsalted butter, melted
- Two ripe bananas, sliced
- Two tablespoons brown sugar

- Cooking spray or additional butter for greasing

Steps:

1. **Preheat** your oven to 350°F (175°C). Grease a baking dish with cooking spray or butter.

2. **combine** the rolled oats, chopped pecans, baking powder, cinnamon, and salt in a large bowl.

3. **whisk together** the milk, maple syrup, eggs, and melted butter in another bowl.

4. **Pour** the wet ingredients into the dry ingredients and **mix** until well combined.

5. **Pour** the mixture into the prepared baking dish, spreading it out evenly.

6. **Arrange** the sliced bananas on top of the oatmeal mixture in a single layer.

7. **Sprinkle** the brown sugar over the bananas.

8. **Bake** in the oven for 30-35 minutes until the oatmeal is set and the edges are golden brown.

9. **Let cool** for a few minutes before serving. Serve warm, and enjoy!

Nutrition Facts (per serving):

- Calories: 320
- Total Fat: 12g
    - Saturated Fat: 3g
    - Trans Fat: 0g
- Cholesterol: 65mg
- Sodium: 220mg

- Total Carbohydrate: 47g
  - Dietary Fiber: 4g
  - Sugars: 24g
- Protein: 8g

SMOKED SALMON BREAKFAST CROISSANTS WITH HERBED CREAM CHEESE

Cooking Time: 15 minutes

Serving: 4

Materials:

- Four croissants
- 200g smoked salmon
- 150g cream cheese, softened
- One tablespoon chopped fresh dill
- One tablespoon chopped fresh chives
- One tablespoon lemon juice
- Salt and pepper to taste
- Arugula leaves (optional, for garnish)

Steps:

1. **Prepare the Herbed Cream Cheese:** In a mixing bowl, combine the softened cream cheese, chopped dill, chopped chives, lemon juice, salt, and pepper. Mix well until all ingredients are fully incorporated. Set aside.

2. **Slice the Croissants:** Slice each in half horizontally, but not all through.

3. **Spread the Herbed Cream Cheese:** Spread a generous amount of the herbed cream cheese on the bottom half of each croissant.

4. **Layer the Smoked Salmon:** Divide the smoked salmon evenly among the croissants, placing it on top of the herbed cream cheese.

5. **Garnish and Serve:** Optionally, garnish each croissant with a few arugula leaves for added freshness. Close each croissant with the top half.

6. **Serve:** Arrange the smoked salmon breakfast croissants on a serving platter and serve immediately.

Nutrition Facts (per serving):

- Calories: 380 kcal
- Total Fat: 23g
    - Saturated Fat: 12g
    - Trans Fat: 0g
- Cholesterol: 70mg
- Sodium: 720mg
- Total Carbohydrates: 28g
    - Dietary Fiber: 1g
    - Sugars: 6g
- Protein: 15g

BREAKFAST BURRITO BOWLS WITH SPICY BLACK BEANS AND FRIED EGGS

Cooking Time: 30 minutes

Servings: 4

Materials:

- One can (15 oz) black beans, drained and rinsed
- One tablespoon olive oil
- One small onion, diced
- Two cloves garlic, minced

- One teaspoon ground cumin
- One teaspoon chilli powder
- Salt and pepper to taste
- Four large eggs
- 4 cups cooked brown rice
- One avocado, sliced
- 1 cup cherry tomatoes, halved
- 1/4 cup chopped fresh cilantro
- Hot sauce (optional)
- Lime wedges for serving

Steps:

1. Heat olive oil in a skillet over medium heat. Add diced onion, minced garlic, and sauté until softened, about 3-4 minutes.

2. Add drained black beans to the skillet with onions and garlic. Stir in ground cumin, chilli powder, salt, and pepper. Cook for another 5-7 minutes until the beans are heated and well coated with the spices.

3. Fend the eggs to your desired doneness in a separate non-stick skillet. Season with salt and pepper.

4. To assemble the burrito bowls, divide cooked brown rice among four. Top each with a portion of the spicy black beans, a fried egg, sliced avocado, cherry tomatoes, and chopped cilantro.

5. Drizzle with hot sauce if desired and serve with lime wedges on the side.

Nutrition Facts (per serving):

- Calories: 450
- Total Fat: 19g
- Saturated Fat: 3.5g

- Cholesterol: 185mg
- Sodium: 260mg
- Total Carbohydrates: 55g
- Dietary Fiber: 13g
- Sugars: 3g
- Protein: 17g

CINNAMON ROLL DUTCH BABY WITH CREAM CHEESE GLAZE

Cooking Time: 30 minutes

Serving: 4

Materials:

- 1 cup all-purpose flour
- 1 cup milk
- Four large eggs
- 1/4 cup granulated sugar
- Two teaspoons vanilla extract
- 1/2 teaspoon ground cinnamon
- 1/4 teaspoon salt
- Four tablespoons unsalted butter
- 1/4 cup brown sugar
- One teaspoon ground cinnamon

Cream Cheese Glaze:

- 4 ounces cream cheese, softened
- 1/2 cup powdered sugar
- 2-3 tablespoons milk
- 1/2 teaspoon vanilla extract

Steps:

1. Preheat your oven to 425°F (220°C). Place a 10-inch cast-iron skillet or oven-safe skillet in the oven to preheat.

2. combine the flour, milk, eggs, granulated sugar, vanilla extract, ground cinnamon, and salt in a blender. Blend until smooth.

3. Once the skillet is preheated, carefully remove it from the oven and add the butter, swirling it around until melted and coating the bottom of the skillet.

4. Quickly pour the batter into the skillet over the melted butter. Return the skillet to the oven and bake for 15-20 minutes or until the Dutch baby is puffed and golden brown.

5. Prepare the cinnamon sugar mixture While the Dutch baby is baking. In a small bowl, mix the brown sugar and ground cinnamon.

6. Once the Dutch baby is done, remove it from the oven and sprinkle the cinnamon sugar mixture evenly over the top.

7. To make the cream cheese glaze, in a medium bowl, beat the softened cream cheese, powdered sugar, milk, and vanilla extract until smooth and creamy.

8. Drizzle the cream cheese glaze over the warm Dutch baby.

9. Slice and serve immediately.

Nutrition Facts (per serving):

- Calories: 398 kcal
- Total Fat: 21g
    - Saturated Fat: 11g
    - Trans Fat: 0g
- Cholesterol: 184mg
- Sodium: 296mg
- Total Carbohydrate: 42g

- Dietary Fiber: 1g
- Sugars: 25g
- Protein: 10g

BREAKFAST PIZZA WITH EGGS, BACON, AND ROASTED TOMATOES

Cooking Time: 25 minutes

Servings: 4

Materials:

- One pre-made pizza dough (store-bought or homemade)
- Four large eggs
- Six slices of bacon, cooked and crumbled
- 1 cup cherry tomatoes, halved
- 1 cup shredded mozzarella cheese
- Two tablespoons olive oil
- Salt and pepper to taste
- Fresh basil leaves for garnish (optional)

Steps:

1. Preheat your oven to 425°F (220°C). Place a baking sheet in the oven to heat up.

2. Roll out the pizza dough on a lightly floured surface to your desired thickness. Transfer the dough to a piece of parchment paper.

3. Heat 1 tablespoon of olive oil over medium heat in a skillet. Add the cherry tomatoes and cook until they soften and caramelize, about 5-7 minutes. Remove from heat and set aside.

4. Brush the pizza dough with the remaining olive oil. Sprinkle half of the shredded mozzarella cheese evenly over the dough.

5. Arrange the cooked bacon and roasted cherry tomatoes over the cheese.

6. Carefully crack the eggs onto the pizza, spacing them evenly. Season with salt and pepper to taste.

7. Sprinkle the remaining mozzarella cheese over the eggs.

8. Carefully transfer the pizza on the parchment paper onto the preheated baking sheet in the oven. Bake for 10-12 minutes until the crust is golden brown and the egg whites are set.

9. Once done, remove the pizza from the oven and let it cool for a couple of minutes before slicing.

10. Garnish with fresh basil leaves if desired, then slice and serve hot.

Nutrition Facts (per serving):

- Calories: 480
- Total Fat: 27g
- Saturated Fat: 9g
- Cholesterol: 225mg
- Sodium: 890mg
- Total Carbohydrate: 34g
- Dietary Fiber: 2g
- Sugars: 2g
- Protein: 24g

BLUEBERRY LEMON RICOTTA PANCAKES WITH BLUEBERRY COMPOTE

Cooking Time: 20 minutes

Serving: 4

Materials:

- 1 cup all-purpose flour
- One tablespoon granulated sugar
- One teaspoon baking powder
- 1/2 teaspoon baking soda
- 1/4 teaspoon salt
- 1 cup ricotta cheese
- 3/4 cup milk
- Two large eggs
- Zest of 1 lemon
- 1 cup fresh blueberries
- Butter or oil for cooking
- **For the Blueberry Compote:**
    - 1 cup fresh or frozen blueberries
    - Two tablespoons granulated sugar
    - One tablespoon lemon juice

Steps:

1. Whisk the flour, sugar, baking powder, baking soda, and salt in a large mixing bowl.

2. whisk together the ricotta cheese, milk, eggs, and lemon zest in another bowl until smooth.

3. Gently fold the wet ingredients into the dry ingredients until combined. Be careful not to overmix; the batter may be slightly lumpy.

4. Gently fold in the fresh blueberries.

5. Heat a non-stick skillet or griddle over medium heat and lightly grease with butter or oil.

6. Pour 1/4 cup of batter onto the skillet for each pancake. Cook until bubbles form on the surface, then flip and cook until golden brown on both sides.

7. Repeat with the remaining batter, greasing the skillet as needed.

8. **For the Blueberry Compote**, combine the blueberries, sugar, and lemon juice in a small saucepan. Cook over medium heat, stirring occasionally, until the blueberries burst and the mixture thickens slightly, about 5-7 minutes.

9. Serve the pancakes warm, topped with blueberry compote.

Nutrition Facts (per serving):

- Calories: 320
- Total Fat: 10g
- Saturated Fat: 5g
- Cholesterol: 120mg
- Sodium: 460mg
- Total Carbohydrate: 45g
- Dietary Fiber: 2g
- Sugars: 15g
- Protein: 13g

SAVOURY SPINACH AND FETA GALETTE WITH A SOFT-BOILED EGG

Cooking Time: 45 minutes

Servings: 4

Materials:

- One pre-made pie crust (store-bought or homemade)
- 4 cups fresh spinach, chopped

- 1 cup crumbled feta cheese
- One small onion, finely chopped
- Two cloves garlic, minced
- One tablespoon olive oil
- Salt and pepper to taste
- Four eggs
- One tablespoon butter, melted
- Optional: red pepper flakes for added heat
- Optional: chopped fresh herbs for garnish (such as parsley or chives)

Steps:

1. Preheat your oven to 375°F (190°C).

2. heat the olive oil over medium heat in a large skillet. Add the chopped onion and minced garlic, sautéing until translucent and fragrant, about 3-4 minutes.

3. Add the chopped spinach to the skillet and cook until wilted, about 2-3 minutes. Season with salt, pepper, and red pepper flakes if desired. Remove from heat and let cool slightly.

4. Roll out the pie crust on a baking sheet lined with parchment paper. Leave about a 2-inch border around the edges.

5. Spread the cooked spinach mixture evenly over the centre of the pie crust, leaving the border clear. Sprinkle the crumbled feta cheese over the spinach.

6. Fold the edges of the pie crust over the filling, creating a rustic, free-form shape. Brush the edges of the crust with melted butter.

7. Crack an egg into each quarter of the galette, keeping the yolks intact. Season the eggs with a pinch of salt and pepper.

8. Bake in the preheated oven for 20-25 minutes, or until the crust is golden brown and the egg whites are set, but the yolks are still runny.

9. Remove from the oven and let cool slightly before serving. Garnish with chopped fresh herbs if desired.

Nutrition Facts (per serving):

- Calories: 320
- Total Fat: 21g
    - Saturated Fat: 8g
- Cholesterol: 220mg
- Sodium: 640mg
- Total Carbohydrates: 21g
    - Dietary Fiber: 2g
    - Sugars: 2g
- Protein: 13g

NUTELLA SWIRL BANANA BREAD FRENCH TOAST STICKS

Cooking Time: 30 minutes

Servings: 4

Materials:

- One loaf of banana bread (store-bought or homemade)
- Three large eggs
- 1/2 cup milk
- One teaspoon vanilla extract
- 1/4 teaspoon ground cinnamon
- Nutella spread
- Butter or cooking spray
- Maple syrup (optional for serving)
- Sliced bananas and berries (optional, for garnish)

Steps:

1. **Prepare Banana Bread:** If using store-bought banana bread, slice it into sticks about 1 inch thick. If making homemade banana bread, let it cool completely before slicing it into sticks.

2. **Make French Toast Mixture:** In a shallow dish, whisk together eggs, milk, vanilla extract, and ground cinnamon until well combined.

3. **Create a Nutella Swirl:** Microwave the Nutella spread for about 30 seconds until it's soft and easy to swirl. Take a butter knife and swirl the Nutella into the banana bread sticks, ensuring each stick has a good amount.

4. **Dip Banana Bread Sticks:** Dip each Nutella-swirled banana bread stick into the egg mixture to coat both sides evenly.

5. **Cook French Toast Sticks:** Melt butter over medium heat in a large skillet or griddle, or use cooking spray to coat the surface. Place the dipped banana bread sticks in the skillet and cook for about 2-3 minutes on each side, or until golden brown and cooked through.

6. **Serve:** Remove the French toast sticks from the skillet and place them on a serving plate. Serve warm with maple syrup drizzled on top and garnish with sliced bananas and berries if desired.

Nutrition Facts:

(NOTE: NUTRITION FACTS MAY VARY DEPENDING ON THE INGREDIENTS AND SERVING SIZES. THE FOLLOWING VALUES ARE APPROXIMATE PER SERVING.)

- Calories: 350
- Total Fat: 15g

- Saturated Fat: 5g
- Cholesterol: 130mg
- Sodium: 300mg
- Total Carbohydrates: 45g
- Dietary Fiber: 2g
- Sugars: 22g
- Protein: 8g

COCONUT BERRY SMOOTHIE BOWL WITH TOASTED COCONUT GRANOLA

Cooking Time: 15 minutes

Serving: 2

Materials:

For the Smoothie Bowl:

- 1 cup mixed berries (strawberries, blueberries, raspberries)
- One ripe banana, frozen
- 1/2 cup coconut milk
- 1/4 cup Greek yogurt
- Two tablespoons shredded coconut
- One tablespoon honey (optional)
- Ice cubes (optional)

For the Toasted Coconut Granola:

- 1 cup rolled oats
- 1/4 cup shredded coconut
- Two tablespoons honey
- Two tablespoons coconut oil
- 1/4 teaspoon vanilla extract
- Pinch of salt

Steps:

1. **Prepare the Smoothie Bowl:**

·In a blender, combine the mixed berries, frozen banana, coconut milk, Greek yoghurt, shredded coconut, and honey (if using).

·Blend until smooth and creamy. If the mixture is too thick, add a few ice cubes and blend again until desired consistency is reached.

·Pour the smoothie into two bowls.

2. **Make the Toasted Coconut Granola:**

·Preheat your oven to 325°F (160°C).

·In a mixing bowl, combine the rolled oats, shredded coconut, honey, melted coconut oil, vanilla extract, and a pinch of salt. Mix well until everything is evenly coated.

·Spread the mixture onto a baking sheet lined with parchment paper.

·Bake for 10-15 minutes or until the granola is golden brown, stirring occasionally to ensure even toasting.

·Once done, remove from the oven and let it cool completely.

3. **Assemble the Smoothie Bowl:**

·Top each smoothie bowl with a generous sprinkle of the toasted coconut granola.

·Optionally, garnish with additional fresh berries and shredded coconut.

·Serve immediately and enjoy!

Nutrition Facts (per serving):

- Calories: 320
- Total Fat: 16g
    - Saturated Fat: 12g
    - Trans Fat: 0g
- Cholesterol: 3mg
- Sodium: 32mg
- Total Carbohydrate: 42g
    - Dietary Fiber: 6g
    - Sugars: 21g
- Protein: 6g
- Vitamin D: 0%
- Calcium: 6%
- Iron: 10%
- Potassium: 17%

BREAKFAST TACOS WITH SPICY CHORIZO AND SCRAMBLED EGGS

Cooking Time: 20 minutes

Servings: 4

Materials:

- Eight small flour or corn tortillas
- Eight large eggs
- 200g spicy chorizo, casing removed and crumbled
- One small onion, diced
- One small bell pepper, diced
- One jalapeño pepper, seeded and diced (optional for extra spice)
- One tablespoon olive oil
- Salt and pepper to taste

- 1 cup shredded cheese (cheddar or Mexican blend)
- Fresh cilantro leaves for garnish
- Salsa, avocado, and sour cream for serving (optional)

Steps:

1. **Prep Ingredients:** Heat the olive oil in a skillet over medium heat. Add diced onions and bell peppers. Sauté until softened, about 3-4 minutes.

2. **Cook Chorizo:** Push the vegetables to one side of the skillet and add the crumbled chorizo. Cook until browned and cooked through, breaking it up with a spoon as it cooks, about 5-6 minutes.

3. **Scramble Eggs:** Beat the eggs with salt and pepper in a separate bowl. Pour the eggs into the skillet with the cooked chorizo and vegetables. Stir gently until the eggs are scrambled and cooked to your desired consistency, about 3-4 minutes.

4. **Warm Tortillas:** While the eggs are cooking, warm the tortillas. You can do this by wrapping them in a damp paper towel and microwaving for 30 seconds or heating them in a dry skillet for about 30 seconds on each side.

5. **Assemble Tacos:** Divide the scrambled egg mixture evenly among the warmed tortillas. Top each taco with shredded cheese and garnish with fresh cilantro leaves.

6. **Serve:** Serve the breakfast tacos with salsa, sliced avocado, and sour cream on the side, if desired.

Nutrition Facts (per serving):

- Calories: 380
- Total Fat: 24g
- Saturated Fat: 9g

- Cholesterol: 390mg
- Sodium: 690mg
- Total Carbohydrate: 21g
- Dietary Fiber: 2g
- Sugars: 2g
- Protein: 21g

CARAMELIZED PEAR DUTCH BABY WITH WHIPPED MASCARPONE

Cooking Time: 30 minutes

Serving: 4

Materials:

- Two ripe pears, peeled, cored, and thinly sliced
- Three tablespoons unsalted butter
- Three large eggs
- ½ cup all-purpose flour
- ½ cup whole milk
- Two tablespoons granulated sugar
- One teaspoon vanilla extract
- Pinch of salt
- Confectioners' sugar for dusting

Whipped Mascarpone:

- ½ cup mascarpone cheese
- ¼ cup heavy cream
- Two tablespoons powdered sugar
- ½ teaspoon vanilla extract

Steps:

1. Preheat your oven to 425°F (220°C).

2. Melt two tablespoons of butter over medium heat in a cast-iron skillet or oven-safe pan. Add the sliced pears and sprinkle with one tablespoon of granulated sugar. Cook, stirring occasionally, until the pears are caramelized and softened, about 5-7 minutes. Remove the pears from the skillet and set aside.

3. combine the eggs, flour, milk, remaining sugar, vanilla extract, and salt in a blender. Blend until smooth.

4. Add the remaining tablespoon of butter to the skillet and let it melt, swirling to coat the bottom and sides.

5. Pour the batter into the skillet over the melted butter.

6. Arrange the caramelized pear slices on top of the batter.

7. Transfer the skillet to the preheated oven and bake for 15-20 minutes until the Dutch baby is puffed and golden brown.

8. While the Dutch baby is baking, prepare the whipped mascarpone. Combine the mascarpone cheese, heavy cream, powdered sugar, and vanilla extract in a mixing bowl. Beat with a hand mixer or whisk until soft peaks form.

9. Once the Dutch baby is done, remove it from the oven and let it cool for a few minutes.

10. Dust the Dutch baby with confectioners' sugar and serve warm with dollops of whipped mascarpone on top.

Nutrition Facts:

- Serving Size: 1 slice (¼ of the Dutch baby)
- Calories: 320
- Total Fat: 20g
- Saturated Fat: 12g
- Cholesterol: 160mg

- Sodium: 120mg
- Total Carbohydrate: 29g
- Dietary Fiber: 2g
- Sugars: 14g
- Protein: 7g

CAPRESE AVOCADO TOAST WITH BALSAMIC GLAZE

Cooking Time: 10 minutes

Servings: 2

Materials:

- Two ripe avocados
- Four slices of whole-grain bread
- One large ripe tomato, sliced
- 1 cup fresh mozzarella, sliced
- Fresh basil leaves
- Balsamic glaze
- Olive oil
- Salt and pepper to taste

Steps:

1. Begin by toasting the slices of whole-grain bread until golden brown.

2. While the bread is toasting, slice the avocados in half and remove the pits. Scoop out the flesh into a small bowl and mash it with a fork until smooth.

3. Once the toast is ready, spread the mashed avocado evenly onto each slice.

4. Layer the avocado toast with slices of ripe tomato and fresh mozzarella.

5. Drizzle balsamic glaze over the top of each toast.

6. Garnish with fresh basil leaves and a sprinkle of salt and pepper.

7. Serve immediately and enjoy!

Nutrition Facts (per serving):

- Calories: 320
- Total Fat: 18g
- Saturated Fat: 6g
- Cholesterol: 22mg
- Sodium: 350mg
- Total Carbohydrates: 30g
- Dietary Fiber: 9g
- Sugars: 6g
- Protein: 12g

LUNCH RECIPES:

THAI PEANUT CHICKEN AND VEGGIE SPRING ROLLS WITH SWEET CHILI SAUCE

Cooking Time: 30 minutes

Serving: Makes about eight spring rolls

Materials:

- 1 cooked chicken breast, shredded
- 1 cup shredded cabbage
- One carrot, julienned
- One red bell pepper, thinly sliced
- 1/4 cup chopped fresh cilantro
- Eight rice paper wrappers
- 1/4 cup creamy peanut butter
- Two tablespoons of soy sauce
- One tablespoon of lime juice
- One tablespoon honey
- One clove of garlic, minced
- One teaspoon of grated ginger
- 1/4 teaspoon red pepper flakes (optional)
- Sweet chili sauce for dipping

Steps:

1. combine shredded chicken, cabbage, carrot, red bell pepper, and cilantro in a bowl. Mix well.

2. prepare the peanut sauce in another bowl by whisking together peanut butter, soy sauce, lime juice, honey, garlic, ginger, and red pepper flakes. If the sauce is too thick, you can thin it with water.

3. Dip one rice paper wrapper into warm water for a few seconds until it softens. Place it on a clean surface.

4. Place a small portion of the chicken and veggie mixture onto the bottom third of the rice paper wrapper.

5. Fold the bottom of the wrapper over the filling, then fold in the sides and roll tightly to enclose the filling.

6. Repeat with the remaining wrappers and filling.

7. Serve the spring rolls with sweet chilli sauce for dipping.

Nutrition Facts (per serving):

- Calories: 180
- Total Fat: 7g
    - Saturated Fat: 1.5g
    - Trans Fat: 0g
- Cholesterol: 20mg
- Sodium: 320mg
- Total Carbohydrate: 20g
    - Dietary Fiber: 2g
    - Sugars: 5g
- Protein: 10g

GRILLED PEACH AND PROSCIUTTO PIZZA WITH HONEY BALSAMIC GLAZE

Cooking Time: 20 minutes

Serving: 4

Materials:

- 1 pound pizza dough, homemade or store-bought

- Two ripe peaches, sliced
- 6 slices of prosciutto
- 1 cup shredded mozzarella cheese
- ¼ cup crumbled goat cheese
- Two tablespoons honey
- Two tablespoons of balsamic glaze
- Olive oil, for brushing
- Salt and pepper to taste
- Fresh basil leaves for garnish

Steps:

1. Preheat your grill to medium-high heat.

2. Roll out the pizza dough on a lightly floured surface to your desired thickness.

3. Brush one side of the dough with olive oil.

4. Carefully place the oiled side of the dough directly onto the grill grates. Grill for 2-3 minutes or until grill marks appear and the dough puffs up. Remove from grill and set aside.

5. Mix the honey and balsamic glaze in a small bowl to create the glaze for the pizza.

6. Flip the grilled side of the dough facing up, and evenly spread the mozzarella cheese over the surface.

7. Arrange the sliced peaches and prosciutto over the cheese.

8. Drizzle the honey balsamic glaze over the Top of the pizza.

9. Sprinkle the crumbled goat cheese evenly over the pizza.

10. Season with salt and pepper to taste.

11. Carefully return the pizza to the grill and cook for 5-7 minutes until the cheese is melted and bubbly and the crust is golden brown.

12. Once done, remove from the grill and let it cool slightly before slicing.

13. Garnish with fresh basil leaves before serving.

Nutrition Facts: (per serving)

- Calories: 380
- Total Fat: 15g
- Saturated Fat: 7g
- Cholesterol: 30mg
- Sodium: 740mg
- Total Carbohydrates: 46g
- Dietary Fiber: 2g
- Sugars: 15g
- Protein: 16g

HARVEST COBB SALAD WITH HONEY MUSTARD VINAIGRETTE

Cooking Time: 20 minutes

Serving: 4

Ingredients:

- 6 cups mixed greens (such as spinach, kale, and arugula)
- 1 cup cooked quinoa
- 1 cup cooked chicken breast, diced
- 1 cup cherry tomatoes, halved
- 1 cup cooked corn kernels
- One avocado, diced
- Four hard-boiled eggs, sliced

- ½ cup crumbled feta cheese
- ¼ cup chopped green onions
- Salt and pepper to taste

Honey Mustard Vinaigrette:

- ¼ cup olive oil
- Two tablespoons of apple cider vinegar
- One tablespoon honey
- One tablespoon of Dijon mustard
- Salt and pepper to taste

Steps:

1. **Prepare the Vinaigrette:** In a small bowl, whisk together olive oil, apple cider vinegar, honey, Dijon mustard, salt, and pepper until well combined. Set aside.

2. **Assemble the Salad:** Arrange the mixed greens as the base in a large salad bowl. Then, arrange cooked quinoa, diced chicken breast, cherry tomatoes, corn kernels, diced avocado, sliced hard-boiled eggs, crumbled feta cheese, and chopped green onions on Top of the greens.

3. **Drizzle with Vinaigrette:** Drizzle the prepared honey mustard vinaigrette over the salad.

4. **Season:** Season the salad with salt and pepper to taste.

5. **Toss and Serve:** Gently toss all the ingredients until well combined and evenly coated with the vinaigrette. Serve immediately.

Nutrition Facts:

- Calories: 380
- Total Fat: 23g

- Saturated Fat: 5g
- Cholesterol: 210mg
- Sodium: 420mg
- Total Carbohydrate: 24g
- Dietary Fiber: 6g
- Sugars: 8g
- Protein: 25g

BBQ CHICKEN QUINOA SALAD WITH AVOCADO AND LIME

Cooking Time: 30 minutes

Serving: 4

Materials:

- 1 cup quinoa, rinsed
- 2 cups water or chicken broth
- Two boneless, skinless chicken breasts
- Salt and pepper to taste
- 1 cup corn kernels (fresh, canned, or frozen)
- One red bell pepper, diced
- 1/4 cup red onion, finely chopped
- 1/4 cup fresh cilantro, chopped
- One avocado, diced
- Juice of 2 limes
- 1/4 cup BBQ sauce
- Two tablespoons olive oil

Steps:

1. **Cook Quinoa:** Bring the water or chicken broth to a boil in a medium saucepan. Stir in the quinoa, reduce heat to low, cover, and simmer for 15-20 minutes, or until the quinoa is cooked and the liquid is absorbed. Fluff with a fork and set aside to cool.

2. **Prepare Chicken:** Season chicken breasts with salt and pepper. Heat a grill pan or skillet over medium-high heat and add a drizzle of olive oil. Cook the chicken breasts for 6-8 minutes per side until cooked and no longer pink in the centre. Remove from heat and rest for a few minutes before slicing into strips.

3. **Assemble Salad:** In a large mixing bowl, combine cooked quinoa, sliced chicken breast, corn kernels, diced red bell pepper, chopped red onion, and chopped cilantro. Toss gently to combine.

4. **Make Dressing:** In a small bowl, whisk together the lime juice, BBQ sauce, and olive oil until well combined.

5. **Add Avocado and Dressing:** Gently fold diced avocado into the salad mixture. Drizzle the dressing over the salad and toss until everything is evenly coated.

6. **Serve:** Divide the BBQ chicken quinoa salad into serving bowls. Garnish with additional cilantro if desired. Serve immediately and enjoy!

Nutrition Facts (per serving):

- Calories: 420
- Total Fat: 17g
- Saturated Fat: 2.5g
- Cholesterol: 45mg
- Sodium: 350mg
- Total Carbohydrate: 44g
- Dietary Fiber: 8g
- Sugars: 7g
- Protein: 26g

MEDITERRANEAN HUMMUS BOWL WITH HERBED PITA CHIPS

Cooking Time: 20 minutes

Servings: 4

Materials:

- Two cans (15 ounces each) chickpeas, drained and rinsed
- Three cloves garlic, minced
- 1/4 cup tahini
- 1/4 cup extra virgin olive oil
- Juice of 1 lemon
- One teaspoon ground cumin
- Salt and pepper to taste
- 1 cup cherry tomatoes, halved
- One cucumber, diced
- 1/2 red onion, thinly sliced
- 1/4 cup Kalamata olives, pitted and halved
- Two tablespoons chopped fresh parsley
- Two tablespoons chopped fresh mint
- Four whole wheat pita bread rounds
- Olive oil cooking spray
- One teaspoon dried oregano
- One teaspoon dried thyme

Steps:

1. combine chickpeas, minced garlic, tahini, olive oil, lemon juice, cumin, salt, and pepper in a food processor. Blend until smooth and creamy, adding water to reach your desired consistency. Adjust seasoning to taste.

2. Transfer the hummus to a serving bowl and set aside.

3. In a separate bowl, combine the cherry tomatoes, cucumber, red onion, Kalamata olives, parsley, and mint. Toss gently to mix.

4. Preheat the oven to 375°F (190°C).

5. Cut each pita bread round into eight wedges. Place the wedges in a single layer on a baking sheet lined with parchment paper.

6. Lightly spray the pita wedges with olive oil cooking spray and sprinkle with dried oregano and thyme.

7. Bake in the oven for 8-10 minutes or until the pita chips are golden and crispy.

8. Arrange the herbed pita chips around the edges of the hummus bowl.

9. Spoon the Mediterranean vegetable mixture into the centre of the hummus.

10. Serve the Mediterranean hummus bowl with herbed pita chips immediately, or cover and refrigerate until ready to serve.

Nutrition Facts (per serving):

- Calories: 385
- Total Fat: 18g
- Saturated Fat: 2g
- Cholesterol: 0mg
- Sodium: 460mg
- Total Carbohydrates: 45g
- Dietary Fiber: 10g
- Sugars: 5g
- Protein: 13g

CALIFORNIA TURKEY CLUB WRAP WITH AVOCADO RANCH DRESSING

Cooking Time: 15 minutes

Serving: 4 wraps

Materials:

- Four large whole wheat or spinach tortillas
- 1 lb cooked turkey breast, thinly sliced
- Eight slices of cooked bacon
- One large ripe avocado, sliced
- 1 cup cherry tomatoes, halved
- 1 cup shredded lettuce
- 1/2 cup shredded cheddar cheese
- 1/4 cup ranch dressing
- One ripe avocado
- Juice of 1/2 lime
- 1/4 cup plain Greek yogurt
- One clove garlic, minced
- Salt and pepper to taste

Steps:

1. **Prepare Avocado Ranch Dressing:** In a blender or food processor, combine the ripe avocado, lime juice, Greek yoghurt, minced garlic, salt, and pepper. Blend until smooth and creamy. Adjust seasoning to taste. Set aside.

2. **Assemble Wraps:** Lay out the tortillas on a clean surface. Spread a tablespoon of the avocado ranch dressing evenly over each tortilla, leaving about an inch border around the edges.

3. Layer the sliced turkey breast, bacon slices, avocado slices, cherry tomatoes, shredded lettuce, and cheddar cheese evenly over the tortillas.

4. **Wrap:** Fold in the sides of each tortilla, then tightly roll up from the bottom to enclose the filling.

5. **Serve:** Slice the wraps in half diagonally and serve immediately, or wrap tightly in foil for an on-the-go meal.

Nutrition Facts (per serving):

- Calories: 480
- Total Fat: 26g
- Saturated Fat: 7g
- Cholesterol: 75mg
- Sodium: 800mg
- Total Carbohydrates: 31g
- Dietary Fiber: 8g
- Sugars: 3g
- Protein: 35g

SPICY SHRIMP SUSHI BOWLS WITH CREAMY SRIRACHA SAUCE

Cooking Time: 25 minutes

Servings: 4

Materials:

- 1 cup sushi rice
- 2 cups water
- 1 pound large shrimp, peeled and deveined
- Two tablespoons soy sauce
- One tablespoon Sriracha sauce
- One tablespoon honey
- One tablespoon sesame oil
- 2 cups mixed vegetables (such as bell peppers, cucumber, avocado, and carrots), thinly sliced
- One tablespoon black sesame seeds (optional)
- Two green onions, thinly sliced

- One nori sheet, cut into thin strips

For Creamy Sriracha Sauce:

- 1/4 cup mayonnaise
- 1 tablespoon Sriracha sauce
- One tablespoon lime juice
- One teaspoon honey

Steps:

1. **Cook Sushi Rice:** Rinse sushi rice under cold water until the water runs clear. Combine rice and water in a rice cooker or a pot. Cook according to the rice cooker instructions or bring to a boil, then reduce heat to low, cover, and simmer for 18-20 minutes, or until rice is tender and water is absorbed. Let it cool slightly.

2. **Prepare Creamy Sriracha Sauce:** In a small bowl, whisk together mayonnaise, Sriracha sauce, lime juice, and honey until smooth. Adjust the amount of Sriracha to your desired level of spiciness. Set aside.

3. **Marinate Shrimp:** In a bowl, combine soy sauce, Sriracha sauce, honey, and sesame oil. Add shrimp and toss to coat. Let it marinate for about 10 minutes.

4. **Cook Shrimp:** Heat a skillet over medium-high heat. Add marinated shrimp and cook for 2-3 minutes per side or until shrimp turn pink and opaque. Remove from heat and set aside.

5. **Assemble Sushi Bowls:** Divide cooked sushi rice among serving bowls. Arrange cooked shrimp and mixed vegetables on Top of the rice. Drizzle with creamy Sriracha sauce.

6. **Garnish:** Sprinkle black sesame seeds, sliced green onions, and nori strips over the bowls for garnish.

7. **Serve:** Serve the Spicy Shrimp Sushi Bowls immediately, and enjoy!

Nutrition Facts:

(PER SERVING)

Calories: 420

Total Fat: 14g

Saturated Fat: 2g

Cholesterol: 180mg

Sodium: 900mg

Total Carbohydrates: 52g

Dietary Fiber: 5g

Sugars: 9g

Protein: 23g

GREEK SALAD WITH GRILLED CHICKEN AND TZATZIKI DRESSING

Cooking Time: 30 minutes

Servings: 4

Materials:

For the Salad:

- Two boneless, skinless chicken breasts
- One large cucumber, diced

- Two large tomatoes, diced
- One red onion, thinly sliced
- One green bell pepper, diced
- 1/2 cup Kalamata olives, pitted
- 4 oz feta cheese, crumbled
- 1/4 cup fresh parsley, chopped
- Salt and pepper to taste
- Olive oil for grilling

For the Tzatziki Dressing:

- 1 cup Greek yogurt
- 1/2 cucumber, grated and squeezed to remove excess moisture
- Two cloves garlic, minced
- One tablespoon fresh lemon juice
- One tablespoon extra virgin olive oil
- One tablespoon chopped fresh dill
- Salt and pepper to taste

Steps:

1. **Prepare the Chicken:** Preheat the grill to medium-high heat. Season chicken breasts with salt, pepper, and a drizzle of olive oil. Grill chicken for 6-7 minutes per side or until cooked through. Remove from grill and let it rest for 5 minutes before slicing.

2. **Make the Tzatziki Dressing:** In a bowl, combine Greek yoghurt, grated cucumber, minced garlic, lemon juice, olive oil, chopped dill, salt, and pepper. Mix well until smooth. Refrigerate until ready to serve.

3. **Assemble the Salad:** In a large mixing bowl, combine diced cucumber, tomatoes, red onion, bell pepper, and Kalamata olives. Toss gently to mix. Add crumbled feta cheese and chopped parsley—season with salt and pepper to taste.

4. **Serve:** Divide the salad among four plates. Top each salad with sliced grilled chicken. Drizzle tzatziki dressing over the chicken and salad. Serve immediately.

Nutrition Facts (per serving):

- Calories: 350
- Total Fat: 18g
    - Saturated Fat: 6g
- Cholesterol: 80mg
- Sodium: 580mg
- Total Carbohydrates: 15g
    - Dietary Fiber: 4g
    - Sugars: 8g
- Protein: 32g

CAPRESE PESTO PASTA SALAD WITH BALSAMIC GLAZE

Cooking Time: 20 minutes

Servings: 4

Materials:

- 8 ounces fusilli pasta
- 1 cup cherry tomatoes, halved
- 1 cup fresh mozzarella balls, halved
- 1/4 cup fresh basil leaves, chopped
- 1/4 cup pine nuts, toasted
- Two tablespoons pesto sauce
- Two tablespoons balsamic glaze
- Salt and pepper to taste
- Optional: fresh basil leaves for garnish

Steps:

1. Cook the fusilli pasta according to package instructions until al dente. Drain and rinse under cold water to stop the cooking process. Let it cool completely.

2. combine the cooked pasta, cherry tomatoes, fresh mozzarella, chopped basil leaves, and toasted pine nuts in a large mixing bowl.

3. Add the pesto sauce to the bowl and toss everything together until the pasta and other ingredients are evenly coated.

4. Season the salad with salt and pepper to taste.

5. Drizzle the balsamic glaze over the salad just before serving.

6. Garnish with fresh basil leaves if desired.

7. Serve chilled or at room temperature.

Nutrition Facts (per serving):

- Calories: 380
- Total Fat: 20g
    - Saturated Fat: 6g
- Cholesterol: 20mg
- Sodium: 280mg
- Total Carbohydrate: 38g
    - Dietary Fiber: 3g
    - Sugars: 4g
- Protein: 15g

VEGGIE SUSHI ROLLS WITH SPICY SRIRACHA MAYO

Cooking Time: 30 minutes

Serving: Makes four rolls

Materials:

- Four sheets of nori (seaweed)
- 2 cups sushi rice, cooked and seasoned
- One small cucumber, julienned
- 1 small carrot, julienned
- One ripe avocado, sliced
- 1/2 red bell pepper, thinly sliced
- Four tablespoons Sriracha mayo
- Soy sauce for dipping

Steps:

1. Lay a bamboo sushi mat on a clean surface. Place a sheet of nori, shiny side down, on the mat.

2. Spread a thin layer of sushi rice evenly over the nori, leaving a small border at the Top.

3. Arrange cucumber, carrot, avocado, and red bell pepper slices in a line across the centre of the rice.

4. Using the bamboo mat, tightly roll the sushi away from you, starting from the edge closest to you. Apply gentle pressure to shape the roll.

5. Repeat with the remaining nori sheets and fillings.

6. Using a sharp knife, slice each roll into 6-8 pieces.

7. Serve the sushi rolls with spicy Sriracha mayo for dipping and soy sauce if desired.

Nutrition Facts:

- Serving Size: 1 roll
- Calories: 210
- Total Fat: 7g
- Saturated Fat: 1g

- Cholesterol: 0mg
- Sodium: 320mg
- Total Carbohydrates: 34g
- Dietary Fiber: 5g
- Sugars: 3g
- Protein: 4g

ROASTED VEGETABLE PANZANELLA SALAD WITH BALSAMIC GLAZE

Cooking Time: 30 minutes

Servings: 4

Materials:

- One medium eggplant, diced
- Two bell peppers (any colour), diced
- One large zucchini, diced
- One red onion, sliced
- 2 cups cherry tomatoes, halved
- 4 cups day-old bread, cubed
- Four cloves garlic, minced
- 1/4 cup olive oil
- Salt and pepper to taste
- 1/4 cup balsamic glaze
- Fresh basil leaves, torn, for garnish

Steps:

1. Preheat your oven to 400°F (200°C).

2. combine the diced eggplant, bell peppers, zucchini, red onion, cherry tomatoes, minced garlic, and cubed bread in a large mixing bowl.

3. Drizzle the olive oil over the vegetables and bread and toss until everything is evenly coated.

4. Spread the mixture in a single layer on a baking sheet lined with parchment paper—season with salt and pepper.

5. Roast in the oven for 20-25 minutes, or until the vegetables are tender and the bread is toasted, stirring halfway through.

6. Once roasted, transfer the mixture to a serving platter.

7. Drizzle the balsamic glaze over the Top of the salad.

8. Garnish with torn fresh basil leaves.

9. Serve immediately as a warm salad or let it cool slightly for a room temperature dish.

Nutrition Facts (per serving):

- Calories: 320
- Total Fat: 12g
- Saturated Fat: 2g
- Cholesterol: 0mg
- Sodium: 350mg
- Total Carbohydrate: 47g
- Dietary Fiber: 7g
- Sugars: 12g
- Protein: 8g

THAI COCONUT CHICKEN AND RICE NOODLE SOUP

Cooking Time: 30 minutes

Serving: 4 servings

Materials:

- One tablespoon vegetable oil
- One onion, thinly sliced
- Two cloves garlic, minced
- One tablespoon ginger, grated
- Two tablespoons Thai red curry paste
- 4 cups chicken broth
- One can (14 oz) coconut milk
- One tablespoon fish sauce
- One tablespoon soy sauce
- One tablespoon brown sugar
- 1 lb chicken breast, thinly sliced
- 4 oz rice noodles
- One red bell pepper, thinly sliced
- 1 cup snap peas
- Juice of 1 lime
- Salt and pepper to taste
- Fresh cilantro and lime wedges for garnish

Steps:

1. Heat vegetable oil in a large pot over medium heat. Add sliced onion, minced garlic, and grated ginger. Sauté until fragrant, about 2 minutes.

2. Stir in Thai red curry paste and cook for another minute.

3. Pour in chicken broth and coconut milk. Bring to a simmer.

4. Add fish sauce, soy sauce, and brown sugar. Stir to combine.

5. Add thinly sliced chicken breast to the pot and simmer for 8-10 minutes until cooked.

6. Meanwhile, cook rice noodles according to package instructions. Drain and set aside.

7. Add sliced red bell pepper and snap peas to the soup. Simmer for another 3-4 minutes until vegetables are tender-crisp.

8. Stir in lime juice and season with salt and pepper to taste.

9. To serve, divide the cooked rice noodles among serving bowls and ladle the hot soup over them.

10. Garnish with fresh cilantro and lime wedges before serving.

Nutrition Facts:

- Serving Size: 1/4 of recipe
- Calories: 420
- Total Fat: 24g
- Saturated Fat: 18g
- Cholesterol: 75mg
- Sodium: 1000mg
- Total Carbohydrate: 22g
- Dietary Fiber: 3g
- Sugars: 8g
- Protein: 30g

CALIFORNIA CHICKEN, AVOCADO, AND BACON SALAD WITH TAHINI DRESSING

Cooking Time: 20 minutes

Serving: 4

Materials:

- Two boneless, skinless chicken breasts
- Salt and pepper to taste
- Six slices of bacon
- 6 cups mixed greens (such as spinach, arugula, and kale)

- Two ripe avocados, sliced
- 1 cup cherry tomatoes, halved
- 1/4 cup crumbled feta cheese
- 1/4 cup sliced almonds, toasted
- **For the Tahini Dressing:**
    - 1/4 cup tahini
    - Two tablespoons lemon juice
    - One tablespoon honey
    - One clove garlic, minced
    - 2-4 tablespoons water (as needed to thin out the dressing)
    - Salt and pepper to taste

Steps:

1. Season the chicken breasts with salt and pepper on both sides.

2. Heat a grill or grill pan over medium-high heat. Grill the chicken breasts for 6-8 minutes per side or until cooked through. Remove from heat and let them rest for a few minutes before slicing.

3. In the same grill pan, cook the bacon until crispy. Once done, transfer to a paper towel-lined plate to drain excess grease. Crumble the bacon into bite-sized pieces.

4. combine the mixed greens, sliced avocado, cherry tomatoes, crumbled bacon, feta cheese, and toasted almonds in a large salad bowl.

5. In a small bowl, whisk together the tahini, lemon juice, honey, minced garlic, salt, and pepper. Gradually add water until the desired consistency is reached.

6. Drizzle the tahini dressing over the salad and toss until evenly coated.

7. Divide the salad onto plates and top each with sliced grilled chicken.

8. Serve immediately and enjoy!

Nutrition Facts:

- Serving Size: 1/4 of the recipe
- Calories: 420
- Total Fat: 29g
  - Saturated Fat: 6g
  - Trans Fat: 0g
- Cholesterol: 70mg
- Sodium: 480mg
- Total Carbohydrates: 20g
  - Dietary Fiber: 9g
  - Sugars: 6g
- Protein: 26g
- Vitamin D: 2%
- Calcium: 10%
- Iron: 15%
- Potassium: 22%

MEDITERRANEAN VEGGIE WRAPS WITH SUN-DRIED TOMATO HUMMUS

Cooking Time: 20 minutes

Serving: 4 wraps

Materials:

- Four whole wheat or spinach tortillas
- 1 cup sun-dried tomatoes (packed in oil), drained
- One can (15 oz) chickpeas, drained and rinsed

- Two cloves garlic, minced
- Two tablespoons tahini
- Juice of 1 lemon
- Two tablespoons olive oil
- Salt and pepper to taste
- 1 cup cucumber, sliced
- 1 cup cherry tomatoes, halved
- 1 cup mixed salad greens
- ½ cup crumbled feta cheese
- ¼ cup sliced kalamata olives
- Fresh parsley leaves for garnish (optional)

Steps:

1. **Prepare the Sun-Dried Tomato Hummus:** In a food processor, combine the sun-dried tomatoes, chickpeas, minced garlic, tahini, lemon juice, olive oil, salt, and pepper. Blend until smooth and creamy, scraping down the sides as needed. Adjust seasoning to taste.

2. **Assemble the Wraps:** Lay the tortillas on a clean surface. Spread a generous amount of sun-dried tomato hummus onto each tortilla, leaving about an inch of border around the edges.

3. **Add the Fillings:** Divide the cucumber slices, cherry tomatoes, mixed salad greens, feta cheese, and kalamata olives evenly among the tortillas, placing the ingredients in the centre of each tortilla.

4. **Wrap the Wraps:** Fold the sides of each tortilla towards the centre, then roll it up tightly from the bottom, enclosing the fillings. Secure with toothpicks if needed.

5. **Serve:** Trim off the ends of each wrap if desired, then slice them in half diagonally. Arrange on a serving platter, garnish with fresh parsley leaves if using, and serve immediately.

Nutrition Facts (per serving):

- Calories: 380
- Total Fat: 18g
  - Saturated Fat: 4g
  - Trans Fat: 0g
- Cholesterol: 11mg
- Sodium: 650mg
- Total Carbohydrate: 45g
  - Dietary Fiber: 8g
  - Sugars: 7g
- Protein: 13g

CAPRESE ORZO PASTA SALAD WITH BASIL VINAIGRETTE

Cooking Time: 20 minutes

Servings: 4

Ingredients:

- 1 cup orzo pasta
- 1 pint cherry tomatoes, halved
- 1 cup fresh mozzarella balls, halved
- 1/4 cup fresh basil leaves, chopped
- Two tablespoons pine nuts, toasted
- Salt and black pepper to taste

Basil Vinaigrette:

- 1/4 cup fresh basil leaves
- 1/4 cup extra virgin olive oil
- Two tablespoons balsamic vinegar
- One clove garlic, minced
- Salt and black pepper to taste

Steps:

1. Cook the orzo pasta according to package instructions until al dente. Drain and rinse under cold water to stop the cooking process. Set aside.

2. combine the cooked orzo pasta, cherry tomatoes, mozzarella balls, chopped basil leaves, and toasted pine nuts in a large bowl.

3. combine the basil leaves, olive oil, balsamic vinegar, minced garlic, salt, and black pepper in a blender or food processor. Blend until smooth.

4. Pour the basil vinaigrette over the pasta salad and toss gently to coat everything evenly.

5. Season with additional salt and black pepper to taste, if needed.

6. Serve immediately or refrigerate for at least 30 minutes to allow the flavours to meld together before serving.

Nutrition Facts:

- Serving Size: 1/4 of recipe
- Calories: 320
- Total Fat: 18g
- Saturated Fat: 5g
- Cholesterol: 20mg
- Sodium: 180mg
- Total Carbohydrates: 31g
- Dietary Fiber: 3g
- Sugars: 4g
- Protein: 10g

GRILLED PEACH, CORN, AND AVOCADO SALAD WITH HONEY LIME VINAIGRETTE

Cooking Time: 20 minutes

Serving: 4

Materials:

- Two peaches, ripe but firm, halved and pitted
- Two ears of corn, husked
- One avocado, sliced
- 6 cups mixed salad greens
- 1/4 cup crumbled feta cheese (optional)
- 1/4 cup chopped fresh cilantro (optional)

For the Honey Lime Vinaigrette:

- Three tablespoons extra virgin olive oil
- Two tablespoons lime juice
- One tablespoon honey
- One teaspoon Dijon mustard
- Salt and pepper to taste

Steps:

1. Preheat the grill to medium-high heat.

2. Brush the peach halves and corn with olive oil to prevent sticking.

3. Grill the peaches and corn until they are tender and have grill marks, about 3-4 minutes per side for the peaches and 8-10 minutes for the corn. Remove from the grill and let cool slightly.

4. Cut the kernels off the corn cobs and place them in a large salad bowl.

5. Slice the grilled peaches and add them to the bowl with the avocado slices and mixed salad greens.

6. If using, sprinkle the crumbled feta cheese and chopped cilantro over the salad.

7. To make the vinaigrette, whisk together the olive oil, lime juice, honey, Dijon mustard, salt, and pepper in a small bowl.

8. Drizzle the vinaigrette over the salad and toss gently to coat.

9. Serve immediately and enjoy!

Nutrition Facts (per serving):

CALORIES: 220

TOTAL FAT: 15g

SATURATED FAT: 2g

CHOLESTEROL: 0mg

SODIUM: 110mg

TOTAL CARBOHYDRATE: 21g

DIETARY FIBER: 5g

TOTAL SUGARS: 11g

PROTEIN: 4g

VITAMIN D: 0mcg

CALCIUM: 60mg

BUFFALO CHICKEN LETTUCE WRAPS WITH BLUE CHEESE DRESSING

Cooking Time: 25 minutes

Servings: 4

Ingredients:

- 1 pound boneless, skinless chicken breast, cooked and shredded
- 1/2 cup buffalo sauce
- One tablespoon olive oil
- One teaspoon garlic powder
- One teaspoon onion powder
- Salt and pepper to taste
- Eight large lettuce leaves (such as iceberg or butter lettuce)
- 1/2 cup crumbled blue cheese
- 1/4 cup Greek yogurt
- Two tablespoons mayonnaise
- One tablespoon lemon juice
- 1/2 teaspoon Worcestershire sauce
- 1/4 teaspoon garlic powder
- Salt and pepper to taste
- Chopped green onions for garnish (optional)

Steps:

1. Heat olive oil over medium heat in a large skillet. Add shredded chicken and buffalo sauce. Stir until chicken is evenly coated and heated through, about 5 minutes.

2. Season the chicken with garlic powder, onion powder, salt, and pepper. Stir well to combine and cook for an additional 2-3 minutes. Remove from heat.

3. To make the blue cheese dressing, mix crumbled blue cheese, Greek yogurt, mayonnaise, lemon juice, Worcestershire sauce, garlic powder, salt, and pepper in a small bowl.

4. spoon some of the buffalo chicken mixture onto each leaf to assemble the lettuce wraps.

5. Drizzle with blue cheese dressing and sprinkle with chopped green onions if desired.

6. Serve immediately and enjoy!

Nutrition Facts: (per serving)

- Calories: 280
- Total Fat: 14g
    - Saturated Fat: 4g
    - Trans Fat: 0g
- Cholesterol: 85mg
- Sodium: 1000mg
- Total Carbohydrate: 4g
    - Dietary Fiber: 1g
    - Sugars: 1g
- Protein: 33g

VIETNAMESE BANH MI SANDWICHES WITH PICKLED VEGETABLES

Cooking Time: 1 hour

Serving: 4 sandwiches

Materials:

For Pickled Vegetables:

- 1 large carrot, julienned
- One medium daikon radish, julienned
- 1/2 cup rice vinegar
- 1/4 cup water

- Two tablespoons sugar
- One teaspoon salt

For Sandwiches:

- 4 Vietnamese baguettes or French rolls
- 1 pound pork tenderloin, thinly sliced
- Two tablespoons soy sauce
- Two cloves garlic, minced
- One tablespoon fish sauce
- One tablespoon vegetable oil
- One cucumber, thinly sliced
- One jalapeno, thinly sliced
- 1/2 cup cilantro leaves
- Four tablespoons mayonnaise
- Sriracha sauce (optional)

Steps:

1. **Prepare Pickled Vegetables:**

·In a small saucepan, combine rice vinegar, water, sugar, and salt. Heat over medium heat until sugar and salt dissolve.

·Place julienned carrot and daikon in a heatproof jar or bowl.

·Pour the vinegar mixture over the vegetables. Let it cool to room temperature, then cover and refrigerate for at least 1 hour before using.

2. **Marinate Pork:**

·In a bowl, mix soy sauce, minced garlic, and fish sauce. Add sliced pork tenderloin and toss to coat. Let it marinate for at least 30 minutes.

3. **Cook Pork:**

- Heat vegetable oil in a skillet over medium-high heat.

- Add the marinated pork slices and cook until browned and cooked through, about 3-4 minutes per side. Remove from heat.

4. **Assemble Sandwiches:**

- Slice the Vietnamese baguettes or French rolls in half lengthwise.

- Spread mayonnaise on one side of each roll.

- Arrange cooked pork slices on the bottom half of each roll.

- Top with pickled vegetables, cucumber, jalapeno, and cilantro leaves.

- Drizzle with Sriracha sauce if desired.

- Close the sandwiches with the top halves of the rolls.

5. **Serve:**

- Serve the Banh Mi sandwiches immediately, or wrap them tightly in parchment paper for later enjoyment.

Nutrition Facts: (per serving)

- Calories: 450
- Total Fat: 14g
- Saturated Fat: 3g
- Cholesterol: 75mg
- Sodium: 950mg
- Total Carbohydrate: 47g
- Dietary Fiber: 4g
- Sugars: 9g
- Protein: 33g

ROASTED TOMATO AND BASIL PESTO GRILLED CHEESE SANDWICHES

Cooking Time: 30 minutes

Serving: 2 sandwiches

Materials:

- Four slices of your favourite bread (sourdough or whole wheat works well)
- 1 cup cherry tomatoes, halved
- Two tablespoons olive oil
- Salt and pepper to taste
- Four tablespoons basil pesto
- 1 cup shredded mozzarella cheese
- Butter for spreading

Steps:

1. **Preheat the oven to 375°F (190°C).**

2. **Roast the Tomatoes:** Place the halved cherry tomatoes on a baking sheet. Drizzle with olive oil, then season with salt and pepper. Toss to coat evenly. Roast in the oven for 15-20 minutes or until the tomatoes are soft and slightly caramelized. Remove from the oven and set aside.

3. **Prepare the Sandwiches:** Spread one side of each bread slice with butter. Flip the slices over, and spread a generous amount of basil pesto on two of them.

4. **Assemble the Sandwiches:** Evenly distribute the roasted cherry tomatoes on the slices with pesto. Sprinkle shredded mozzarella cheese over the tomatoes, then place the remaining bread slices on Top, buttered side facing outwards.

5. **Grill the Sandwiches:** Heat a skillet or griddle over medium heat. Carefully place the assembled sandwiches onto the skillet or griddle. Cook for about 3-4 minutes on each side until the bread is golden brown and the cheese is melted.

6.**Serve:** Once the sandwiches are grilled to perfection, remove them from the heat. If desired, cut each sandwich in half diagonally and serve hot.

Nutrition Facts (per serving):

- Calories: 420
- Total Fat: 25g
- Saturated Fat: 9g
- Cholesterol: 35mg
- Sodium: 640mg
- Total Carbohydrate: 35g
- Dietary Fiber: 5g
- Sugars: 5g
- Protein: 15g

CHIPOTLE CHICKEN AND AVOCADO QUINOA SALAD WITH HONEY LIME VINAIGRETTE

Cooking Time: 30 minutes

Servings: 4

Materials:

- 1 cup quinoa, rinsed
- 2 cups water or chicken broth
- Two boneless, skinless chicken breasts
- One tablespoon olive oil
- One teaspoon chipotle powder

- Salt and pepper to taste
- One avocado, diced
- 1 cup cherry tomatoes, halved
- 1/2 cup corn kernels (fresh, canned, or frozen)
- 1/4 cup chopped fresh cilantro
- 1/4 cup crumbled feta cheese (optional)

For the Honey Lime Vinaigrette:

- 1/4 cup olive oil
- Two tablespoons lime juice
- One tablespoon honey
- One teaspoon Dijon mustard
- Salt and pepper to taste

Steps:

1. **Cook Quinoa:** Bring the water or chicken broth to a boil in a medium saucepan. Add the quinoa, reduce heat to low, cover, and simmer for about 15 minutes or until the quinoa is cooked and liquid is absorbed. Remove from heat and let it cool.

2. **Prepare Chicken:** While the quinoa is cooking, season the chicken breasts with chipotle powder, salt, and pepper. Heat olive oil in a skillet over medium-high heat. Cook the chicken breasts for 6-8 minutes per side or until cooked through. Remove from heat and let them rest for a few minutes before slicing.

3. **Make Vinaigrette:** In a small bowl, whisk together the olive oil, lime juice, honey, Dijon mustard, salt, and pepper until well combined. Set aside.

4. **Assemble Salad:** In a large mixing bowl, combine the cooked quinoa, diced avocado, cherry tomatoes, corn kernels, and chopped cilantro. Add the sliced chipotle chicken. If using, sprinkle the crumbled feta cheese over the Top.

5. **Drizzle with Vinaigrette:** Pour the honey lime vinaigrette over the salad and gently toss until evenly coated.

6. **Serve:** Divide the salad among serving plates or bowls. Garnish with additional cilantro or lime wedges if desired. Enjoy!

Nutrition Facts:

- Serving Size: 1/4 of recipe
- Calories: 460
- Total Fat: 24g
- Saturated Fat: 3.5g
- Cholesterol: 60mg
- Sodium: 240mg
- Total Carbohydrates: 39g
- Dietary Fiber: 7g
- Sugars: 9g
- Protein: 26g

DINNER RECIPES

ONE-PAN MOROCCAN CHICKEN WITH COUSCOUS AND CHICKPEAS

Cooking Time: 45 minutes

Serving: 4 servings

Materials:

- 4 boneless, skinless chicken breasts
- 1 cup couscous
- One can (15 oz) chickpeas, drained and rinsed
- One onion, finely chopped
- Three cloves garlic, minced
- One bell pepper, chopped
- Two tomatoes, diced
- 2 cups chicken broth
- Two tablespoons of olive oil
- One tablespoon Moroccan spice blend (or a mix of cumin, coriander, paprika, cinnamon, and ginger)
- Salt and pepper to taste
- Fresh cilantro leaves for garnish

Steps:

1. Season the chicken breasts with salt, pepper, and half of the Moroccan spice blend.

2. Heat olive oil in a large skillet over medium-high heat. Add the seasoned chicken breasts and cook until browned on both sides, about 3-4 minutes per side. Remove the chicken from the skillet and set aside.

3. In the same skillet, add the chopped onion, minced garlic, and bell pepper. Cook until softened, about 3-4 minutes.

4. Stir in diced tomatoes, chickpeas, couscous, and the remaining Moroccan spice blend. Cook for another 2 minutes, stirring occasionally.

5. Pour in chicken broth and bring to a simmer. Nestle the browned chicken breasts into the skillet, cover, and cook for 15-20 minutes or until the chicken is cooked through and the couscous is tender.

6. Once cooked, remove from heat and let it sit covered for 5 minutes.

7. Garnish with fresh cilantro leaves before serving.

Nutrition Facts (per serving):

- Calories: 430 kcal
- Protein: 35g
- Carbohydrates: 42g
- Fat: 13g
- Saturated Fat: 2g
- Cholesterol: 80mg
- Sodium: 730mg
- Fiber: 7g
- Sugar: 5g

CREAMY GARLIC BUTTER TUSCAN SHRIMP WITH SPINACH AND SUN-DRIED TOMATOES

Cooking Time: 25 minutes

Serving: 4 servings

Ingredients:

- 1 pound large shrimp, peeled and deveined
- Two tablespoons of olive oil
- Four cloves garlic, minced
- 1/2 cup sun-dried tomatoes, chopped
- 1 cup spinach leaves
- 1 cup heavy cream
- 1/2 cup grated Parmesan cheese
- Salt and pepper to taste
- Two tablespoons butter
- Fresh parsley for garnish

Steps:

1. **Prepare Ingredients:** Start by preparing all the ingredients. Peel and devein the shrimp if not already done. Mince the garlic, chop the sun-dried tomatoes, and wash the spinach leaves.

2. **Sauté Shrimp:** Heat olive oil in a large skillet over medium-high heat. Add the shrimp to the skillet and season with salt and pepper. Cook the shrimp on each side for 2-3 minutes until pink and cooked through. Remove the shrimp from the skillet and set aside.

3. **Make the Sauce:** In the same skillet, add butter and minced garlic. Sauté the garlic until fragrant, about 1 minute. Add the chopped sun-dried tomatoes and cook for 2 minutes.

4. **Add Cream and Cheese:** Pour in the heavy cream and grated Parmesan cheese. Stir well to combine. Let the sauce simmer for 2-3 minutes until it thickens slightly.

5. **Add Spinach and Shrimp:** Add the spinach leaves to the skillet and stir until they wilt. Return the cooked shrimp to the skillet and toss everything together until the shrimp is coated in the creamy sauce.

6. **Serve:** Remove the skillet from heat once the shrimp is heated and the spinach is wilted. Taste and adjust seasoning with salt and pepper if needed. Garnish with fresh parsley.

Nutrition Facts (per serving):

- Calories: 380
- Total Fat: 28g
    - Saturated Fat: 14g
- Cholesterol: 236mg
- Sodium: 490mg
- Total Carbohydrates: 10g
    - Dietary Fiber: 2g
    - Sugars: 4g
- Protein: 25g

SHEET PAN HONEY GARLIC CHICKEN AND VEGGIES

Cooking Time: 35 minutes

Servings: 4

Materials:

- Four boneless, skinless chicken breasts
- 4 cups mixed vegetables (such as broccoli florets, bell peppers, and carrots), chopped
- Three tablespoons olive oil
- Salt and pepper, to taste
- Four cloves garlic, minced
- ¼ cup honey
- Two tablespoons of soy sauce
- One tablespoon of rice vinegar
- One teaspoon of sesame oil
- One tablespoon cornstarch

- Sesame seeds, for garnish (optional)
- Chopped green onions for garnish (optional)

Steps:

1. Preheat your oven to 400°F (200°C) and line a large baking sheet with parchment paper or aluminium foil.

2. In a small bowl, whisk together minced garlic, honey, soy sauce, rice vinegar, sesame oil, and cornstarch until well combined. Set aside.

3. Place the chicken breasts in the centre of the prepared baking sheet and arrange the mixed vegetables around the chicken.

4. Drizzle olive oil over the chicken and vegetables, then season with salt and pepper according to your taste.

5. Pour the honey garlic sauce over the chicken and vegetables, ensuring everything is evenly coated.

6. Bake in the preheated oven for about 20-25 minutes, stirring halfway through, until the chicken is cooked through and the vegetables are tender.

7. Once cooked, remove from the oven and let it rest for a few minutes.

8. Sprinkle with sesame seeds and chopped green onions for garnish, if desired, before serving.

Nutrition Facts (per serving):

- Calories: 380
- Total Fat: 14g
    - Saturated Fat: 2.5g
    - Trans Fat: 0g

- Cholesterol: 90mg
- Sodium: 490mg
- Total Carbohydrate: 28g
  - Dietary Fiber: 4g
  - Sugars: 20g
- Protein: 35g

SPAGHETTI CARBONARA WITH CRISPY PROSCIUTTO AND PEAS

Cooking Time: 20 minutes

Serving: 4 servings

Materials:

- 12 ounces spaghetti
- Four large eggs
- 1 cup grated Parmesan cheese, plus more for serving
- Eight slices prosciutto
- 1 cup frozen peas, thawed
- Four cloves garlic, minced
- Salt and freshly ground black pepper to taste
- Two tablespoons of olive oil
- Chopped fresh parsley for garnish

Steps:

1. Cook the spaghetti according to package instructions until al dente. Drain and reserve 1/2 cup of pasta water.

2. whisk together the eggs and grated Parmesan cheese in a bowl. Set aside.

3. Heat olive oil over medium heat in a large skillet. Add minced garlic and cook until fragrant, about 1 minute.

4. Tear the prosciutto into bite-sized pieces and add them to the skillet. Cook until crispy, about 3-4 minutes. Remove from the skillet and set aside.

5. In the same skillet, add the thawed peas and cook for 2-3 minutes until heated through.

6. Add the cooked spaghetti to the skillet with the peas and toss to combine.

7. Remove the skillet from heat and quickly pour in the egg and cheese mixture, stirring constantly to coat the pasta. If the sauce seems too thick, add a splash of reserved pasta water to thin it out.

8. Season with salt and freshly ground black pepper to taste.

9. Serve the spaghetti carbonara topped with crispy prosciutto pieces, chopped fresh parsley, and extra grated Parmesan cheese.

Nutrition Facts:

(PER SERVING)

Calories: 480

Fat: 20g

Carbohydrates: 46g

Protein: 28g

Fiber: 3g

Sugar: 2g

Sodium: 840mg

HONEY SRIRACHA GLAZED SALMON WITH SESAME NOODLES

Cooking Time: 25 minutes

Servings: 4

Materials:

For the Salmon:

- Four salmon fillets (about 6 ounces each)
- 1/4 cup honey
- Two tablespoons of Sriracha sauce
- Two tablespoons of soy sauce
- Two cloves garlic, minced
- One tablespoon of sesame oil
- Salt and pepper to taste
- Sesame seeds for garnish
- Sliced green onions for garnish

For the Sesame Noodles:

- 8 ounces of noodles (such as soba or spaghetti)
- Two tablespoons of sesame oil
- Two tablespoons of soy sauce
- One tablespoon of rice vinegar
- One tablespoon honey
- One teaspoon of grated ginger
- Two cloves garlic, minced
- One tablespoon of sesame seeds
- Sliced green onions for garnish

Steps:

1. **Preheat Oven:** Preheat your oven to 400°F (200°C).

2. **Prepare the Glaze:** In a small bowl, whisk together the honey, Sriracha sauce, soy sauce, minced garlic, and sesame oil until well combined.

3. **Marinate the Salmon:** Place the salmon fillets in a shallow dish or a resealable plastic bag. Pour half of the honey Sriracha glaze over them, ensuring they are evenly coated. Reserve the other half of the glaze for later. Allow the salmon to marinate for about 10-15 minutes.

4. **Prepare the Sesame Noodles:** Cook the noodles according to the instructions until al dente. Drain and rinse under cold water. Whisk together the sesame oil, soy sauce, rice vinegar, honey, grated ginger, minced garlic, and sesame seeds in a large bowl. Add the cooked noodles to the bowl and toss until well-coated. Set aside.

5. **Cook the Salmon:** Place the marinated salmon fillets on a baking sheet lined with parchment paper or lightly greased foil. Season with salt and pepper to taste. Bake in the oven for 12-15 minutes until the salmon is cooked and flakes easily with a fork.

6. **Glaze the Salmon:** During the last 5 minutes of cooking, brush the remaining honey Sriracha glaze over the salmon fillets. Return the salmon to the oven and continue baking until the glaze is caramelized and sticky.

7. **Serve:** Divide the sesame noodles among serving plates. Top each plate with a glazed salmon fillet. Garnish with sesame seeds and sliced green onions. Serve immediately.

Nutrition Facts (per serving):

- Calories: 450 kcal
- Total Fat: 18g
- Saturated Fat: 3.5g
- Cholesterol: 70mg

- Sodium: 900mg
- Total Carbohydrates: 39g
- Dietary Fiber: 2g
- Sugars: 18g
- Protein: 32g

CAJUN SHRIMP AND GRITS WITH ANDOUILLE SAUSAGE

Cooking Time: 25 minutes

Servings: 4

Materials:

For Salmon:

- Four salmon fillets (about 6 oz each), skinless
- 1/4 cup honey
- Two tablespoons of Sriracha sauce
- Two tablespoons of soy sauce
- Two cloves garlic, minced
- One tablespoon of sesame oil
- Salt and pepper to taste
- Sesame seeds for garnish
- Sliced green onions for garnish

For Sesame Noodles:

- 8 oz (about 230g) noodles (such as soba or spaghetti)
- Two tablespoons of sesame oil
- Two tablespoons of soy sauce
- One tablespoon of rice vinegar
- One tablespoon honey
- One tablespoon of sesame seeds
- Two green onions, thinly sliced
- One tablespoon of chopped cilantro (optional)

Steps:

1. **Preheat Oven**: Preheat your oven to 400°F (200°C). Line a baking sheet with parchment paper.

2. **Prepare Salmon Glaze**: In a small bowl, whisk together honey, Sriracha sauce, soy sauce, minced garlic, sesame oil, salt, and pepper.

3. **Glaze the Salmon**: Place the salmon fillets on the prepared baking sheet. Gently brush the honey Sriracha glaze over them.

4. **Bake Salmon**: Bake the salmon in the oven for 12-15 minutes, or until the salmon is cooked and flakes easily with a fork.

5. **Cook Noodles**: While baking salmon, cook the noodles according to package instructions until al dente. Drain and rinse under cold water. Set aside.

6. **Prepare Sesame Noodles**: In a large bowl, whisk together sesame oil, soy sauce, rice vinegar, and honey. Add the cooked noodles to the bowl and toss until well-coated. Sprinkle sesame seeds, sliced green onions, and chopped cilantro over the noodles. Toss to combine.

7. **Serve**: Divide the sesame noodles among plates. Top each serving with a glazed salmon fillet. Garnish with additional sesame seeds and sliced green onions if desired. Serve hot.

Nutrition Facts (per serving):

- Calories: 480
- Total Fat: 20g
- Saturated Fat: 3.5g
- Cholesterol: 75mg
- Sodium: 950mg
- Total Carbohydrate: 38g

- Dietary Fiber: 2g
- Sugars: 17g
- Protein: 36g

TERIYAKI CHICKEN STIR-FRY WITH VEGETABLES AND RICE

Cooking Time: 30 minutes

Servings: 4

Materials:

- 1 lb (450g) boneless, skinless chicken breasts, thinly sliced
- Two tablespoons of vegetable oil
- 1 cup broccoli florets
- One bell pepper, thinly sliced
- One carrot, julienned
- 1 cup snap peas, trimmed
- Three cloves garlic, minced
- One teaspoon of ginger, minced
- ½ cup teriyaki sauce
- Two tablespoons of soy sauce
- 2 cups cooked rice
- Salt and pepper, to taste
- Sesame seeds and green onions for garnish

Steps:

1. **Prepare Ingredients:** Thinly slice the chicken breasts and prepare the vegetables as directed.

2. **Cook Chicken:** Heat one tablespoon of vegetable oil in a large skillet over medium-high heat. Add the sliced chicken breasts until

browned and cooked, about 5-6 minutes. Remove the chicken from the skillet and set aside.

3. **Stir-Fry Vegetables:** Heat the remaining tablespoon of vegetable oil in the same skillet. Add the broccoli, bell pepper, carrot, and snap peas. Stir-fry for 3-4 minutes until the vegetables are tender yet crisp.

4. **Add Aromatics:** Add the minced garlic and ginger to the skillet with the vegetables. Stir-fry for another minute until fragrant.

5. **Combine Sauce:** Pour the teriyaki sauce and soy sauce into the skillet. Return the cooked chicken to the skillet and toss everything together until well coated in the sauce. Cook for an additional 2-3 minutes until heated through.

6. **Serve:** Divide the cooked rice among serving plates. Top with the teriyaki chicken stir-fry and vegetables. Garnish with sesame seeds and sliced green onions.

7. **Enjoy:** Serve hot and enjoy your delicious Teriyaki Chicken Stir-Fry with Vegetables and Rice!

Nutrition Facts (per serving):

- Calories: 380
- Total Fat: 10g
- Saturated Fat: 2g
- Cholesterol: 65mg
- Sodium: 1100mg
- Total Carbohydrate: 43g
- Dietary Fiber: 4g
- Sugars: 12g
- Protein: 29g

CREAMY SUN-DRIED TOMATO CHICKEN PARMESAN

Cooking Time: 30 minutes

Serving: 4

Materials:

- Four boneless, skinless chicken breasts
- Salt and pepper to taste
- One tablespoon of olive oil
- 1 cup sun-dried tomatoes, chopped
- Three cloves garlic, minced
- 1 cup heavy cream
- 1 cup grated Parmesan cheese
- One teaspoon of dried basil
- ½ teaspoon dried oregano
- ½ teaspoon crushed red pepper flakes (optional)
- Fresh basil leaves for garnish
- Cooked pasta or rice for serving

Steps:

1. Season the chicken breasts with salt and pepper on both sides.

2. Heat olive oil in a large skillet over medium-high heat. Add the chicken breasts and cook for 6-7 minutes on each side or until golden brown and cooked through. Remove the chicken from the skillet and set aside.

3. add the chopped sun-dried tomatoes and minced garlic in the same skillet. Sauté for 2-3 minutes until the garlic is fragrant.

4. Reduce the heat to medium-low. Pour in the heavy cream and stir to combine with the sun-dried tomatoes and garlic.

5. Add the grated Parmesan cheese, dried basil, dried oregano, and crushed red pepper flakes (if using). Stir until the cheese is melted and the sauce is smooth and creamy.

6. Return the cooked chicken breasts to the skillet, spooning some of the creamy sun-dried tomato sauce over the top.

7. Allow the chicken to simmer in the sauce for 2-3 minutes to heat through and absorb the flavours.

8. Garnish with fresh basil leaves before serving.

9. Serve the Creamy Sun-Dried Tomato Chicken Parmesan hot overcooked pasta or rice.

Nutrition Facts (per serving):

- Calories: 520
- Total Fat: 30g
    - Saturated Fat: 15g
    - Trans Fat: 0g
- Cholesterol: 160mg
- Sodium: 780mg
- Total Carbohydrates: 15g
    - Dietary Fiber: 3g
    - Sugars: 6g
- Protein: 47g

BEEF AND BROCCOLI RAMEN STIR-FRY WITH GARLIC BUTTER SAUCE

Cooking Time: 20 minutes

Serving: 4

Materials:

- Two packs of ramen noodles
- 1 lb (450g) beef sirloin, thinly sliced
- 2 cups broccoli florets
- Three tablespoons soy sauce
- 2 tablespoons oyster sauce
- Two tablespoons butter
- Four cloves garlic, minced
- One tablespoon of brown sugar
- One tablespoon of sesame oil
- Salt and pepper to taste
- Green onions, chopped (for garnish)
- Sesame seeds (for garnish)

Steps:

1. Cook the ramen noodles according to package instructions. Drain and set aside.

2. In a bowl, mix soy sauce, oyster sauce, brown sugar, and sesame oil. Set aside.

3. Heat a large skillet or wok over medium-high heat. Add one tablespoon of butter and let it melt.

4. Add minced garlic to the skillet and sauté for 30 seconds until fragrant.

5. Add the sliced beef to the skillet and stir-fry until browned and cooked, about 3-4 minutes.

6. Remove the beef from the skillet and set aside.

7. In the same skillet, add another tablespoon of butter. Add broccoli florets and stir-fry for 2-3 minutes until slightly tender.

8. Return the cooked beef to the skillet with the broccoli.

9. Pour the sauce mixture over the beef and broccoli. Stir well to coat everything evenly. Cook for another 2 minutes.

10. Add the cooked ramen noodles to the skillet. Toss everything together until the noodles are heated and coated with the sauce.

11. Season with salt and pepper to taste.

12. Garnish with chopped green onions and sesame seeds before serving.

Nutrition Facts (per serving):

- Calories: 480
- Total Fat: 18g
    - Saturated Fat: 8g
    - Trans Fat: 0g
- Cholesterol: 80mg
- Sodium: 1350mg
- Total Carbohydrates: 46g
    - Dietary Fiber: 3g
    - Sugars: 4g
- Protein: 33g

CAPRESE STUFFED CHICKEN WITH BALSAMIC GLAZE

Cooking Time: 30 minutes

Servings: 4

Materials:

- Four boneless, skinless chicken breasts
- Salt and pepper to taste
- Two medium tomatoes, sliced
- 8 oz fresh mozzarella cheese, sliced

- 1/4 cup fresh basil leaves
- Two tablespoons balsamic glaze
- Toothpicks

Steps:

1. Preheat your oven to 375°F (190°C).

2. Season the chicken breasts with salt and pepper on both sides.

3. Slice a pocket into the side of each chicken breast, careful not to cut all the way through.

4. Stuff each chicken breast with sliced tomatoes, mozzarella cheese, and fresh basil leaves, dividing evenly among the breasts.

5. Secure the pockets closed with toothpicks to hold the filling inside.

6. Heat a skillet over medium-high heat and add a drizzle of olive oil.

7. Once the skillet is hot, sear the stuffed chicken breasts on each side for 2-3 minutes until golden brown.

8. Transfer the seared chicken breasts to a baking dish and bake in the oven for 20-25 minutes until the chicken is cooked and no longer pink in the centre.

9. Remove the toothpicks before serving.

10. Drizzle the cooked chicken breasts with balsamic glaze before serving.

Nutrition Facts (per serving):

- Calories: 320
- Total Fat: 12g

- Saturated Fat: 6g
- Cholesterol: 110mg
- Sodium: 380mg
- Total Carbohydrates: 6g
  - Dietary Fiber: 1g
  - Sugars: 4g
- Protein: 45g

GARLIC BUTTER MUSHROOM RISOTTO WITH PEAS AND PARMESAN

Cooking Time: 30 minutes

Servings: 4

Materials:

- 1 cup Arborio rice
- 4 cups vegetable or chicken broth
- Two tablespoons olive oil
- Two tablespoons butter
- One small onion, finely chopped
- Three cloves garlic, minced
- 8 oz mushrooms, sliced (button or cremini)
- 1 cup frozen peas
- ½ cup grated Parmesan cheese
- Salt and pepper to taste
- Fresh parsley, chopped (for garnish, optional)

Steps:

1. **Prepare the Broth:** Heat the vegetable or chicken broth in a saucepan over low heat, keeping it warm throughout the cooking process.

2. **Sauté Onions and Garlic:** Heat olive oil and one tablespoon of butter over medium heat in a large skillet or saucepan. Add chopped onions, minced garlic, and sauté until softened and fragrant for about 2-3 minutes.

3. **Cook Mushrooms:** Add sliced mushrooms to the skillet. Cook until they are golden brown and tender, about 5-7 minutes. Season with salt and pepper to taste.

4. **Toast the Rice:** Stir in Arborio rice, coating each grain with the oil and butter mixture. Toast the rice for about 2 minutes until it becomes slightly translucent.

5. **Add Broth:** Add warm broth to the rice mixture, one ladleful at a time. Stir frequently and allow the rice to absorb the broth before adding more. Continue this process until the rice is creamy and cooked, about 18-20 minutes.

6. **Incorporate Peas:** When the rice is almost cooked, stir in the frozen peas. Cook for 2-3 minutes until the peas are heated through.

7. **Finish with Butter and Parmesan:** Remove it from the heat once the risotto reaches the desired consistency (creamy but not too runny). Stir in the remaining tablespoon of butter and grated Parmesan cheese. Adjust seasoning with salt and pepper if needed.

8. **Serve:** Garnish the Garlic Butter Mushroom Risotto with chopped parsley if desired. Serve hot, and enjoy!

Nutrition Facts (per serving):

- Calories: 340 kcal
- Fat: 12g
    - Saturated Fat: 5g
- Carbohydrates: 47g
    - Fiber: 3g

- Sugars: 3g
- Protein: 11g
- Cholesterol: 19mg
- Sodium: 890mg

ONE-POT CREAMY LEMON CHICKEN AND ASPARAGUS ORZO

Cooking Time: 30 minutes

Servings: 4

Materials:

- 1 lb (450g) chicken breast, diced
- One bunch asparagus, trimmed and cut into bite-sized pieces
- 2 cups (400g) orzo pasta
- 4 cups (1 liter) chicken broth
- 1 cup (240ml) heavy cream
- One lemon (zest and juice)
- Four cloves garlic, minced
- One onion, finely chopped
- Two tablespoons olive oil
- Salt and pepper to taste
- Fresh parsley for garnish
- Grated Parmesan cheese (optional)

Steps:

1. Heat olive oil in a large pot over medium-high heat. Add diced chicken breast and cook until browned on all sides, about 5-6 minutes. Remove the chicken from the pot and set aside.

2. In the same pot, add chopped onion and minced garlic. Sauté until onion becomes translucent, about 2-3 minutes.

3. Add orzo pasta to the pot and toast it lightly for about 2 minutes, stirring constantly.

4. Pour in chicken broth and bring to a simmer. Cook for about 10 minutes or until the orzo is almost tender.

5. Stir in heavy cream, lemon zest, lemon juice, and cooked chicken. Allow the mixture to simmer for another 5 minutes, stirring occasionally.

6. Add the asparagus pieces to the pot and cook for 3-4 minutes until the asparagus is tender-crisp and the orzo is cooked through. Season with salt and pepper to taste.

7. Remove from heat and garnish with freshly chopped parsley and grated Parmesan cheese if desired.

Nutrition Facts:

- Serving Size: 1/4 of recipe
- Calories: 600
- Total Fat: 24g
    - Saturated Fat: 10g
- Cholesterol: 120mg
- Sodium: 800mg
- Total Carbohydrate: 56g
    - Dietary Fiber: 4g
    - Sugars: 5g
- Protein: 38g

CHIPOTLE LIME SALMON TACOS WITH MANGO SALSA

Cooking Time: 25 minutes

Servings: 4

Materials:

- Four salmon fillets
- Two chipotle peppers in adobo sauce, minced
- Two tablespoons lime juice
- Two tablespoons olive oil
- Salt and pepper to taste
- Eight small flour or corn tortillas
- One mango, diced
- One small red onion, finely chopped
- One jalapeño, seeded and minced
- 1/4 cup fresh cilantro, chopped
- Juice of 1 lime
- Salt to taste
- Optional toppings: shredded cabbage, avocado slices, sour cream, lime wedges

Steps:

1. Preheat your grill to medium-high heat. If you don't have a grill, preheat your oven to 400°F (200°C) and line a baking sheet with parchment paper.

2. In a small bowl, mix the minced chipotle peppers, lime juice, olive oil, salt, and pepper. Brush this mixture over the salmon fillets, coating them evenly.

3. Place the salmon fillets on the grill or the prepared baking sheet if using the oven. Grill or bake for 4-5 minutes per side until the salmon is cooked and flakes easily with a fork.

4. While the salmon is cooking, prepare the mango salsa. Combine the diced mango, chopped red onion, minced jalapeño, chopped cilantro, lime juice, and salt in a medium bowl. Toss gently to combine.

5. Warm the tortillas on the grill or in a dry skillet over medium heat for 30 seconds until they're soft and pliable.

6. Once the salmon is cooked, remove it from the grill or oven and let it cool slightly. Use a fork to flake the salmon into bite-sized pieces.

7. To assemble the tacos, place some flaked salmon onto each tortilla, then top with a spoonful of mango salsa. Add any optional toppings you like, such as shredded cabbage, avocado slices, sour cream, or a squeeze of lime juice.

8. Serve immediately and enjoy!

Nutrition Facts (per serving):

NOTE: NUTRITIONAL VALUES MAY VARY DEPENDING ON SPECIFIC INGREDIENTS AND OPTIONAL TOPPINGS.

- Calories: 380
- Total Fat: 16g
    - Saturated Fat: 2.5g
    - Trans Fat: 0g
- Cholesterol: 85mg
- Sodium: 350mg
- Total Carbohydrates: 27g
    - Dietary Fiber: 3g
    - Sugars: 9g
- Protein: 30g

CREAMY SPINACH AND ARTICHOKE STUFFED CHICKEN

Cooking Time: 45 minutes

Servings: 4

Materials:

- Four boneless, skinless chicken breasts
- 1 cup frozen chopped spinach, thawed and drained
- 1 cup canned artichoke hearts, drained and chopped
- 1/2 cup cream cheese, softened
- 1/4 cup grated Parmesan cheese
- Two cloves garlic, minced
- One tablespoon olive oil
- Salt and pepper to taste
- Toothpicks

Steps:

1. Preheat your oven to 375°F (190°C).

2. combine the chopped spinach, chopped artichoke hearts, cream cheese, Parmesan cheese, minced garlic, salt, and pepper in a mixing bowl. Mix well until all ingredients are evenly incorporated.

3. Lay the chicken breasts flat on a cutting board. Using a sharp knife, carefully slice a pocket into each chicken breast, careful not to cut all the way through.

4. Stuff each chicken breast with the spinach and artichoke mixture, dividing it evenly among them. Secure the openings with toothpicks to prevent the filling from spilling out during cooking.

5. Heat olive oil in a large oven-safe skillet over medium-high heat. Once hot, add the stuffed chicken breasts to the skillet and sear for 2-3 minutes on each side until golden brown.

6. Transfer the skillet to the preheated oven and bake for 20-25 minutes until the chicken is cooked and no longer pink in the centre.

7. Once cooked, remove the skillet from the oven and allow the chicken to rest for a few minutes before serving.

8. Serve the creamy spinach and artichoke stuffed chicken hot, optionally garnished with additional Parmesan cheese and chopped parsley.

Nutrition Facts (per serving):

- Calories: 320
- Total Fat: 18g
- Saturated Fat: 8g
- Cholesterol: 120mg
- Sodium: 520mg
- Total Carbohydrates: 6g
- Dietary Fiber: 2g
- Sugars: 2g
- Protein: 34g

SPICY SAUSAGE AND PEPPERONI PIZZA WITH GARLIC BUTTER CRUST

Cooking Time: 20 minutes

Serving: 4

Materials:

- One pre-made pizza dough
- 1/2 cup pizza sauce
- 1 cup shredded mozzarella cheese
- 1/2 cup sliced pepperoni
- 1/2 cup cooked spicy sausage, crumbled
- Two tablespoons butter, melted
- Two cloves garlic, minced
- 1/2 teaspoon Italian seasoning
- Red pepper flakes (optional)
- Fresh basil leaves for garnish (optional)

Steps:

1. Preheat your oven to 450°F (230°C). Place a pizza stone or baking sheet in the oven while it preheats.

2. Roll out the pizza dough on a floured surface to your desired thickness.

3. Mix the melted butter, minced garlic, and Italian seasoning in a small bowl.

4. Roll the dough out onto parchment paper. Brush the garlic butter mixture evenly over the dough, including the edges.

5. Spread the pizza sauce over the garlic-buttered crust.

6. Sprinkle the shredded mozzarella cheese evenly over the sauce.

7. Layer the sliced pepperoni and crumbled spicy sausage on the cheese.

8. If desired, sprinkle some red pepper flakes for extra spice.

9. Carefully transfer the pizza (with the parchment paper) onto the preheated pizza stone or baking sheet in the oven.

10. Bake for 12-15 minutes until the crust is golden brown and the cheese is bubbly and melted.

11. Once done, remove the pizza from the oven and let it cool for a minute or two.

12. Garnish with fresh basil leaves if desired, then slice and serve hot.

Nutrition Facts:

NOTE: NUTRITIONAL VALUES ARE APPROXIMATE AND MAY VARY DEPENDING ON THE INGREDIENTS USED.

- Calories: 380 per serving
- Total Fat: 20g
- Saturated Fat: 10g
- Cholesterol: 55mg
- Sodium: 850mg
- Total Carbohydrates: 32g
- Dietary Fiber: 2g
- Sugars: 3g
- Protein: 16g

THAI COCONUT PEANUT CHICKEN SATAY WITH SPICY PEANUT SAUCE

Cooking Time: 30 minutes

Serving: 4

Materials:

- 1 lb boneless, skinless chicken breasts cut into strips
- 1 cup coconut milk
- ½ cup creamy peanut butter
- Two tablespoons soy sauce
- Two tablespoons lime juice
- Two tablespoons brown sugar
- Two cloves garlic, minced
- One teaspoon ground coriander
- One teaspoon ground cumin
- ½ teaspoon turmeric
- ½ teaspoon chilli powder
- Salt and pepper to taste
- Bamboo skewers soaked in water

- Chopped peanuts and chopped cilantro for garnish (optional)

For the Spicy Peanut Sauce:

- ¼ cup creamy peanut butter
- Two tablespoons soy sauce
- One tablespoon sriracha sauce
- One tablespoon lime juice
- One tablespoon brown sugar
- Two tablespoons water

Steps:

1. Mix coconut milk, peanut butter, soy sauce, lime juice, brown sugar, minced garlic, coriander, ground cumin, turmeric, chilli powder, salt, and pepper to make the marinade.

2. Add the chicken strips to the marinade, ensuring they are fully coated. Cover and refrigerate for at least 1 hour or overnight for best results.

3. Preheat the grill or grill pan over medium-high heat.

4. Thread the marinated chicken strips onto the soaked bamboo skewers.

5. Grill the chicken skewers for 3-4 minutes per side until cooked and slightly charred.

6. While the chicken is grilling, prepare the spicy peanut sauce. Combine peanut butter, soy sauce, sriracha sauce, lime juice, brown sugar, and water in a small saucepan. Heat over medium heat, stirring constantly, until smooth and heated through. Remove from heat and set aside.

7. Once the chicken skewers are done, remove them from the grill and arrange on a serving platter.

8. Drizzle the spicy peanut sauce over the chicken skewers or serve it on the side for dipping.

9. Garnish with chopped peanuts and cilantro if desired. Serve hot and enjoy!

Nutrition Facts:

NOTE: NUTRITION INFORMATION MAY VARY DEPENDING ON INGREDIENTS USED AND PORTION SIZES.

- Calories: 450
- Total Fat: 28g
- Saturated Fat: 12g
- Cholesterol: 75mg
- Sodium: 860mg
- Total Carbohydrates: 16g
- Dietary Fiber: 3g
- Sugars: 9g
- Protein: 35g

HONEY GARLIC BUTTER SHRIMP AND BROCCOLI WITH RICE

Cooking Time: 25 minutes

Servings: 4

Materials:

- 1 lb (450g) large shrimp, peeled and deveined
- 2 cups broccoli florets
- Three cloves garlic, minced
- Three tablespoons honey
- Two tablespoons soy sauce
- Two tablespoons unsalted butter

- One tablespoon olive oil
- Salt and pepper to taste
- Cooked rice for serving
- Optional: sesame seeds and sliced green onions for garnish

Steps:

1. **Prepare Ingredients:** Thaw shrimp if frozen. Pat dry with paper towels and season lightly with salt and pepper. Cut broccoli into small florets. Mince garlic cloves.

2. **Cook Rice:** Start by cooking rice according to package instructions. Keep warm until serving.

3. **Sauté Shrimp:** Heat olive oil over medium-high heat in a large skillet. Add shrimp to the skillet and cook on each side for 2-3 minutes until pink and opaque. Remove shrimp from the skillet and set aside.

4. **Cook Broccoli:** In the same skillet, add a bit more olive oil if needed and add broccoli florets. Sauté for about 3-4 minutes until tender-crisp.

5. **Prepare Sauce:** Lower the heat to medium-low. Add minced garlic to the skillet and cook for about 1 minute until fragrant. Stir in honey and soy sauce, then add butter. Stir until the butter is melted and the sauce is well combined.

6. **Combine Ingredients:** Return the cooked shrimp to the skillet, tossing them in the sauce. Add the sautéed broccoli to the skillet as well. Toss everything together until evenly coated with the honey garlic butter sauce.

7. Serve the Honey Garlic Butter Shrimp and Broccoli over cooked rice. If desired, garnish with sesame seeds and sliced green onions.

Nutrition Facts (per serving):

- Calories: 320
- Total Fat: 12g
  - Saturated Fat: 4g
  - Trans Fat: 0g
- Cholesterol: 190mg
- Sodium: 730mg
- Total Carbohydrate: 27g
  - Dietary Fiber: 2g
  - Sugars: 14g
- Protein: 26g

BALSAMIC GLAZED STEAK ROLLS WITH PROVOLONE AND BASIL

Cooking Time: 30 minutes

Serving: 4 servings

Materials:

- Four thin slices of flank steak (about 6 ounces each)
- Salt and pepper to taste
- Four slices of provolone cheese
- Eight large basil leaves
- 1/4 cup balsamic glaze
- Toothpicks
- Olive oil for cooking

Steps:

1. **Prepare the Steak:** Lay the flank steak slices on a flat surface. Season both sides with salt and pepper.

2. **Layer Ingredients:** Place a slice of provolone cheese on each steak slice, followed by two basil leaves on top of the cheese.

3. **Roll the Steak:** Starting from one end, tightly roll up each steak slice with the cheese and basil inside. Secure the rolls with toothpicks to prevent them from unravelling.

4. **Cook the Rolls:** Heat a drizzle of olive oil in a skillet over medium-high heat. Carefully place the steak rolls in the skillet, seam-side down. Cook for 3-4 minutes on each side until the steak is cooked to your desired level of doneness and the cheese is melted.

5. **Glaze with Balsamic:** Once the steak rolls are cooked, drizzle them with Balsamic glaze while still in the skillet. Allow them to cook for another minute, flipping once, to slightly caramelize the glaze.

6. **Serve:** Remove the toothpicks from the steak rolls before serving. Serve the rolls hot, garnished with extra basil leaves if desired.

Nutrition Facts (per serving):

- Calories: 320
- Total Fat: 18g
- Saturated Fat: 8g
- Cholesterol: 95mg
- Sodium: 320mg
- Total Carbohydrates: 6g
- Dietary Fiber: 0g
- Sugars: 4g
- Protein: 33g

CREAMY LEMON GARLIC BUTTER SALMON WITH ASPARAGUS

Cooking Time: 25 minutes

Serving: 4

Materials:

- Four salmon fillets (about 6 ounces each)
- One bunch of asparagus, ends trimmed
- Four cloves garlic, minced
- 1/4 cup unsalted butter
- 1/2 cup heavy cream
- Two tablespoons lemon juice
- One teaspoon lemon zest
- Salt and pepper to taste
- Fresh chopped parsley for garnish

Steps:

1. Preheat your oven to 400°F (200°C). Line a baking sheet with parchment paper.

2. Place the trimmed asparagus on the prepared baking sheet. Drizzle with olive oil and season with salt and pepper. Toss to coat evenly. Spread them out in a single layer.

3. Season the salmon fillets with salt and pepper on both sides. Place them on the baking sheet with the asparagus.

4. In a skillet, melt the butter over medium heat. Add minced garlic and cook until fragrant, about 1 minute.

5. Pour in the heavy cream, lemon juice, and lemon zest. Stir well to combine. Let it simmer for 2-3 minutes until it thickens slightly.

6. Pour the creamy lemon garlic butter sauce over the salmon fillets, ensuring they are well coated.

7. Bake in the oven for 12-15 minutes or until the salmon is cooked and flakes easily with a fork.

8. While the salmon is baking, roast the asparagus in the oven for 10-12 minutes or until tender but still crisp.

9. Once cooked, remove the salmon and asparagus from the oven. Garnish the salmon with fresh chopped parsley.

10. Serve the creamy lemon garlic butter salmon with roasted asparagus.

Nutrition Facts:

(PER SERVING)

Calories: 480

Total Fat: 32g

- Saturated Fat: 16g
- Cholesterol: 160mg
- Sodium: 190mg
- Total Carbohydrates: 5g
- Dietary Fiber: 2g
- Sugars: 1g
- Protein: 42g

PESTO CHICKEN AND SUMMER VEGETABLE SHEET PAN GNOCCHI

Cooking Time: 30 minutes

Servings: 4

Materials:

- Four boneless, skinless chicken breasts
- 1 pound store-bought gnocchi
- 1 cup cherry tomatoes, halved
- One medium zucchini, sliced
- One medium yellow squash, sliced
- 1/2 cup store-bought pesto sauce
- Two tablespoons olive oil
- Salt and pepper to taste
- Grated Parmesan cheese for garnish (optional)

Steps:

1. Preheat your oven to 400°F (200°C).

2. combine the chicken breasts, cherry tomatoes, zucchini, and yellow squash in a large mixing bowl. Drizzle with olive oil and season with salt and pepper. Toss until everything is evenly coated.

3. Spread the chicken and vegetable mixture evenly on a large baking sheet lined with parchment paper.

4. Place the gnocchi in the same mixing bowl (there is no need to wash them) and add the pesto sauce. Toss until the gnocchi is well coated with the pesto.

5. Arrange the pesto-coated gnocchi on the baking sheet around the chicken and vegetables.

6. Bake in the preheated oven for 20-25 minutes, until the chicken is cooked, the vegetables are tender, and the gnocchi is golden brown.

7. Once done, remove it from the oven and let it cool for a few minutes.

8. Serve the Pesto Chicken and Summer Vegetable Sheet Pan Gnocchi hot, garnished with grated Parmesan cheese if desired.

Nutrition Facts: NOTE: NUTRITION FACTS MAY VARY DEPENDING ON THE BRANDS AND INGREDIENTS USED.

- Serving Size: 1/4 of the recipe
- Calories: 480
- Total Fat: 18g
- Saturated Fat: 4g
- Cholesterol: 95mg
- Sodium: 740mg
- Total Carbohydrate: 40g
- Dietary Fiber: 4g
- Sugars: 3g
- Protein: 38g

CONCLUSION

As we conclude our delightful culinary journey together, I hope this cookbook has stimulated your imagination and motivated you to try new flavours and cooking methods. The cooking process is about satisfying our hunger, creating a sense of fulfilment, and building happy memories with our dear ones. Whether you have prepared a warm and comforting meal on a weekday, hosted a festive celebration, or relished a delicious dessert, I hope these recipes have brought joy and satisfaction to your dining table.

Remember, the beauty of cooking is that it has infinite possibilities, and you can experiment with various ingredients and techniques to create your unique dishes. Keep exploring, experimenting, and, most importantly, sharing your culinary creations with your loved ones. Cooking is an art that requires patience, passion, and creativity, so don't be afraid to try new things and push your boundaries. I wish you many more delicious and exciting culinary adventures ahead!

Printed in Great Britain
by Amazon